English
A Changing Medium for
Education

NEW PERSPECTIVES ON LANGUAGE AND EDUCATION
Series Editor: Professor Viv Edwards, *University of Reading, Reading, UK*
Series Advisor: Professor Allan Luke, *Queensland University of Technology, Brisbane, Australia*

Two decades of research and development in language and literacy education have yielded a broad, multidisciplinary focus. Yet education systems face constant economic and technological change, with attendant issues of identity and power, community and culture. This series will feature critical and interpretive, disciplinary and multidisciplinary perspectives on teaching and learning, language and literacy in new times.

Full details of all the books in this series and of all our other publications can be found on http://www.multilingual-matters.com, or by writing to Multilingual Matters, St Nicholas House, 31–34 High Street, Bristol BS1 2AW, UK.

English
A Changing Medium
for Education

Edited by
Constant Leung and Brian V. Street

MULTILINGUAL MATTERS
Bristol • Buffalo • Toronto

Library of Congress Cataloging in Publication Data
A catalog record for this book is available from the Library of Congress.
English a Changing Medium for Education/Edited by Constant Leung and Brian V. Street.
New Perspectives on Language and Education: 26
Includes bibliographical references and index.
1. English language—Study and teaching—Foreign speakers. 2. Second language acquisition. I. Leung, Constant, II. Street, Brian V.
PE1128.A2E464 2012
428.0071–dc23 2012009345

British Library Cataloguing in Publication Data
A catalogue entry for this book is available from the British Library.

ISBN-13: 978-1-84769-771-4 (hbk)
ISBN-13: 978-1-84769-770-7 (pbk)

Multilingual Matters
UK: St Nicholas House, 31–34 High Street, Bristol BS1 2AW, UK.
USA: UTP, 2250 Military Road, Tonawanda, NY 14150, USA.
Canada: UTP, 5201 Dufferin Street, North York, Ontario M3H 5T8, Canada.

The policy of Multilingual Matters/Channel View Publications is to use papers that are natural, renewable and recyclable products, made from wood grown in sustainable forests. In the manufacturing process of our books, and to further support our policy, preference is given to printers that have FSC and PEFC Chain of Custody certification. The FSC and/or PEFC logos will appear on those books where full certification has been granted to the printer concerned.

Typeset by Techset Composition Ltd., Salisbury, UK.
Printed and bound in Great Britain by the MPG Books Group.

Contents

Contributors

Denise Beale Denise Beale taught English and languages in Victorian schools for many years before completing a prize-winning PhD thesis in 2009 which examined federal government policy to promote computers in Australian schools. She is currently working on two research projects in the Faculty of Education, Monash University, which explore the challenges social media present to schools and the role of vocational education and training in achieving social inclusion for migrant women living in regional Australia.

Martin Dewey Martin Dewey is based at King's College London, where he lectures in Sociolinguistics, World Englishes, Teacher Education, and provides PhD supervision in areas related to the globalization of English and English language teaching. His primary research focus is English as a lingua franca (ELF), exploring, in particular, the implications of ELF for language pedagogy. Most recently this has involved reconsidering contemporary conceptions of knowledge and expertise in teacher education. He has written and presented extensively on empirical research in this field, and is co-author with Alessia Cogo of *Analyzing English as a Lingua Franca: A corpus-driven investigation* (Continuum, 2012).

Bruce Horner Bruce Horner is Endowed Chair in Rhetoric and Composition at the University of Louisville. His recent work investigates the relationship between US college composition, world Englishes, English as a global lingua franca, and the 'English Only' movement. His books include *Cross-Language Relations in Composition*, co-edited with Min-Zhan Lu and Paul Kei Matsuda, and *Terms of Work for Composition: A Materialist Critique*, recipient of the W. Ross Winterowd Award for the Most Outstanding Book in Composition Theory. 'English Only and U.S. College Composition', an essay co-authored with John Trimbur, won the Richard Braddock Award.

Constant Leung Constant Leung is Professor of Educational Linguistics in the Department of Education and Professional Studies at King's College London. He also serves as Deputy Head of Department. His research interests include additional/second language curriculum, language assessment, language education in ethnically and linguistically diverse societies, language policy, and teacher professional development. He is Associate Editor for *Language Assessment Quarterly* and Editor of Research Issues for *TESOL Quarterly*.

Angel Lin Angel Lin received her Ph.D. from the Ontario Institute for Studies in Education, University of Toronto, Canada. She is currently an Associate Professor and Associate Dean in the Faculty of Education, The University of Hong Kong. Angel Lin is well-respected for her versatile, interdisciplinary intellectual scholarship in language and identity studies, bilingual education, classroom discourse analysis, and youth cultural studies. She has published six research books and over seventy research articles and book chapters. She serves on the editorial boards of international research journals including: *Applied Linguistics, British Educational Research Journal, International Journal of Bilingual Education and Bilingualism, Language and Education, Journal of Critical Discourse Studies, and Pragmatics and Society.*

Heather Lotherington Heather Lotherington is Professor of Multilingual Education at York University where she teaches in the Faculty of Education, and in the Graduate Program in Linguistics and Applied Linguistics. Her research focuses on multimodal literacies, multilingual inclusion and pedagogical innovation. Since she spearheaded a collaborative research venture between York University and Joyce Public School in Toronto in 2003, researchers and teachers have been continuously engaged in co-designing multimodal literacies projects (see www.multiliteracies4kidz.ca <http://www.multiliteracies4kidz.ca>). Their award winning research has been widely published. Professor Lotherington's most recent book is: Pedagogy of multiliteracies: Rewriting Goldilocks (Routledge, 2011).

Min-Zhan Lu Min-Zhan Lu is Professor of English and University Scholar at the University of Louisville. She has authored and co-authored books on the problematics of cross cultural and cross linguistic meaning-making in research on and the teaching of reading-writing. She is the recipient of the Richard Braddock Award for her 'Essay on the Work of Composition: Composing English against the Order of Fast Capitalism', and the Mina Shaughnessy Award for her essay 'A Critique of the Politics of Linguistic Innocence'.

Mastin Prinsloo Mastin Prinsloo teaches and researches in Applied Language and Literacy Studies. He is an Associate Professor in the School of Education at the University of Cape Town and he convenes the Masters programmes in Education at UCT. His research has included the study of the literacy practices of adults without schooling in South Africa; literacy in pre-colonial southern Africa; early childhood literacy and school literacy in South Africa; and new media/digital literacies and learning. His co-edited books include *The Social Uses of Literacy* (1996); *Literacies, Local and Global* (2008); and *The Future of Literacy Studies* (2009).

Natalia Sinitskaya Ronda Natalia Sinitskaya Ronda received her PhD in education from York University, Toronto, Canada. Her research focuses on digital literacies broadly defined, particularly the use of new digital spaces for literacy development. In her dissertation Dr Sinitskaya Ronda focuses on digital literacies in online social networking environments. For this research, she designed and programmed an educational application on the popular social networking platform, Facebook. This application was used with a group of linguistically and culturally diverse learners in order to investigate how informal digital spaces can be conceptualized and used in school-based literacy instruction.

Ilana Snyder Ilana Snyder is a Professor in the Faculty of Education, Monash University. Her research has investigated the changes to literacy practices associated with the use of digital technologies. Books that explore the changes include *Hypertext* (1996), *Page to Screen* (1997) and *Silicon Literacies* (2002). In *The Literacy Wars* (2008), she discusses the politics of the volatile media debates around literacy education in Australia. Her most recent books, both co-edited with John Nieuwenhuysen, are *Closing the Gap in Education?* (2010), which considers the education of marginalised peoples and communities in southern world societies, and *A Home Away From Home?* (2011) which explores the complexities of international education in globalising times.

Brian Street Brian Street is Emeritus Professor of Language in Education at King's College, London University and Visiting Professor of Education in the Graduate School of Education, University of Pennsylvania. He has a commitment to linking ethnographic-style research on the cultural dimension of language and literacy with contemporary practice in education and in development. Over the past 25 years he has undertaken anthropological field research and been consultant to projects in these fields in countries of both the North and South (e.g. Nepal, S. Africa, India, USA, UK). He has published 18 books and 120 scholarly papers.

Preface

Constant Leung and Brian Street

The widespread use of English as a preferred medium for schooling in a variety of educational contexts in different parts of the world has given rise to questions about what counts as 'Standard English' and 'literacy'. In relation to both of these questions, the dominant focus in educational contexts has been to assume that English, both spoken and written, is a stable and uniform phenomenon and that teaching has simply to ignore, or to marginalize, everyday or 'popular' uses. However, recent debates in the fields of English (as a school and university subject), English as a Lingua Franca, English as an Additional/Second Language, multimodal communication World Englishes, and in the fields of New Literacy Studies and Academic Literacies, for instance, have shown that English, whether spoken or written, is not a single monolithic language in terms of genre, lexicogrammatical properties and pragmatic conventions of use. Rather, participants in the specific contexts of both community activities and also of classroom curricula can shape both form and function of English in decisive ways, particularly in the light of the increasing use of interactive digital communication devices. This complex view of English is clearly an important issue for language education policy and practice in different world locations.

It is also sometimes assumed that English is a set of neutral linguistic resources and that the adoption of English as a medium for schooling is based on good common sense – an obvious thing to do, so to speak. The choice of English as a preferred medium is, however, a deliberate act involving value judgments and ideological and political principles, whether one is talking about the education of ethnolinguistic minority students in English-speaking countries, or the adoption of English as the official school medium in places such as Singapore or South Africa, where English is one of the many local/ official languages. Recent studies in bi/multilingual interaction in school and elsewhere suggest that the role and utility of English in education has to be understood with reference to the presence, the conferred status and the use of other languages in school and in wider society.

This edited volume is designed to provide a scholarly and research-based discussion on how English in education can be (re)conceptualized and understood in light of the dynamic and changing nature of English. It will cover, inter alia, the following aspects of English (in alphabetical order):

- *Classroom English models* (Leung & Street, Chapter 1; Lin, Chapter 5; Lotherington & Ronda, Chapter 6).
- *Communicative competence in and through English* (Leung & Street, Chapter 1).
- *Cultures in and through English* (Prinsloo, Chapter 2; Snyder & Beale, Chapter 3).
- *Ethnicity and English* (Snyder & Beale, Chapter 3; Prinsloo, Chapter 2).
- *Labels and categories in English Language Teaching* (ELT): *Critical examination of EAL* (English as an Additional Language), *EFL* (English as a Foreign Language), *ELF* (English as a Lingua Franca), *ESL* (English as a Second Language), *ELL* (English Language Learning) (Dewey, Chapter 7; Horner & Lu, Chapter 4).
- *Language/s in English* (Horner & Lu, Chapter 4; Prinsloo, Chapter 2).
- *Literacy in English curricula* (Leung & Street, Chapter 1; Lotherington & Ronda, Chapter 6).
- *Principles of English language policies in education* (Snyder & Beale, Chapter 3; Prinsloo, Chapter 2).
- *Student identity in and through English* (Horner & Lu, Chapter 4; Snyder & Beale, Chapter 3).
- *Teacher professional knowledge of English in context* (Lin, Chapter 5; Lotherington & Ronda, Chapter 6).
- *Technology, literacies and English* (Lotherington & Ronda, Chapter 6).

As the authors in this collection indicate, there are several competing/conflicting views of language and of literacy, which creates tension in how different aspects are conceptualized. It is perhaps more obvious from a social practice perspective, for instance, that what counts as 'English' will vary with context, than it would be from a more formal standard or autonomous language viewpoint, which focuses on the features of language itself, particularly syntax, lexis and phonology, and generalizes what is 'proper' language use from descriptions of these features. From that view English can be described in terms of a set of stable features. In the field of literacy studies, for instance, the models of literacy as a single unified standard, 'autonomous' of social context, have been distinguished from models of literacies, in the plural, as social practices, where what counts as literacy in a given context is already heavily laden with ideological meaning. The tension between these models and their enactment in policy and practice is especially apparent as institutions attempt to prescribe what counts as 'standard' uses of reading and writing, whilst social practices perspectives recognize that such value judgments vary with context and with ideological positions. The concept of 'practice' is central to many of the discussions in this volume as it is regarded as 'situated'. This is not to support complete relativism but rather to acknowledge the complexity and variety of language and literacy in actual practice, and to recognize that judgments need to be based on a context-sensitive perspective – as Hymes (e.g. 1972, 1977, 1994) might argue, what is 'appropriate' for particular purposes – rather than trying to lay down a universal general 'standard'. From this perspective, then, the variations that the authors describe as now to be observed in uses and meanings of 'English' require researchers, as well as practitioners and policy-makers, to both describe the varieties they encounter and to make explicit the criteria for judgments as to which will count for particular purposes. In a sense this is a de-centering exercise. In the Academic Literacies field, for instance, this social practice perspective has led to closer attention being paid to the varieties of genres and styles that are called upon in different disciplines and at different stages of academic work, rather than imposing a single uniform criterion for performance across the board. The Academic Literacies perspective, however, also has to meet and negotiate with the 'Standard English' perspective of what counts as writing, especially in the fields of English for Academic Purposes, English as an Addition/ Foreign/Second Language, English Language Learning (or ELL, particularly in the United States), where traditionally the aim has been to inculcate learners into a single entity called English. Similarly, research in the field of English as a Lingua Franca has strongly suggested that lingua franca use often involves linguistic reformulations and pragmatic innovations that depart from the putative standard variety of English. At the same time, of course, the standard variety itself has many manifestations in the form of Standard American English or General American, Standard British English and Standard Australian English and so on, so in fact both those who have tended towards the 'standard' model and those who advocate the more varied social practice model recognize variation. The authors in the present volume, then, take full account of the tensions between these perspectives and provide detailed and rich accounts of the complexity and variety to be identified in English as it is enacted in spoken and written forms across different contexts, both internationally and within institutions in given situations. As we now talk about multiple literacies, so many of the authors in the present volume recognize the need to take account of multiple Englishes and their enactments in spoken and written media.

The volume begins with an account by the editors, Constant Leung and Brian Street, entitled 'English in the Curriculum – Norms and Practices' that both summarizes the main theoretical approaches in the field and offers classroom examples that illustrate the changes they have noted. Drawing in particular on the work of Hymes (e.g. 1972, 1977, 1994) and Halliday (e.g. 1973, 1975, 2004) they note how the idea of language in communication was taken up by practitioners in the field of English language studies to develop what has become known as 'communicative competence'. In reviewing and updating this concept, in the light of English as a changing medium of education, they provide a vignette drawn from research in an ethnolinguistically diverse London school that gives the reader a glimpse of the potential yield of looking at English as part of social and language practice and that helps set the scene for the discussions by subsequent authors in the volume. English is seen as a set of linguistic resources that can be used for communication, often in combination with actions and other symbolic means. Partly driven by curriculum subject content and woven into classroom activities, it can take a variety of forms (e.g. spoken, written, print, digital), and can serve as the main conveyor of meaning or as a framing facility to draw attention to graphic and other forms of meaning representation. Above all, in addition to being a means for individual meaning-making, English is seen as a carrier of cultural capital and social values, access to which is not equally distributed amongst the different groups of participants in education. Taken as a whole the chapters in the volume, similarly drawing upon specific concrete case studies in a variety of international contexts and developing a theoretically informed and 'practice' minded discussion of English as it is changing, can help us build a rich and more complex picture than the more norm-driven language and literacy approaches that have dominated both research and pedagogy in English.

We summarize briefly here the other chapters in the volume and indicate how the authors draw upon the issues discussed above in their accounts, from many different countries, of the changing nature of English as both spoken and written language.

Chapter 2, 'What Counts as English?', by Mastin Prinsloo draws on data from South Africa to demonstrate the diversity of English that is hidden in the term 'English' in policy construction, arguing along with ourselves and other authors in this volume that the concept of language is by no means neutral. The chapter examines the divergences between what educational policy calls for in South African schools with regard to language and learning and what actually takes place in schools. Drawing on an examination of language policy statements in South Africa and on school-based ethnographic data, Prinsloo develops an analysis that starts to account for the difference between language policy imperatives and schooling practices. And, again like other authors, he takes South African education policy as an example of how constructs to do with language in education policy rely on familiar but problematic ideas about language, development and nation building. He draws in particular on interactional sociolinguistic and ethnographic research, approaches that study language as situated social practice. From this perspective he argues the term 'English', or any other named language, is misleading shorthand for a diverse range of language varieties, genres, registers and practices. He takes us through a variety of policy statements in post-apartheid South Africa, analyzing them in terms of a social practice perspective and showing what is lacking. He then provides a number of ethnographic-style studies of classroom literacy and language practices that demonstrate the limitations of the policy claims. There is, in reality, an acute contrast between the 'English' being taught and used in post-foundation phase classrooms, where the majority of black, ethnic minority students are to be found, and that being taught in suburban schools, where the teachers see the school as an extension and elaboration of the students' home communities' ways of knowing and being, a perspective that is reflected in the language of the classroom. Whilst there are also black and ethnic minority pupils here, the approach is an assimilationist one that edges them towards dominant 'English'. Prinsloo's argument, then, in his discussion of the data from these different classrooms is that 'English' is something different in different school settings, depending on the situated resources and intentions of social actors (see Chapter 3 for a discussion of an Australian context). Effective policy-making, then, should be based on a closer understanding of how language is practiced, rather than relying on projections of romanticized and essentialized notions of language-culture and indigeneity onto particular 'languages'.

Chapter 3, 'The Rise and Rise of English: The Politics of Bilingual Education in Australia's Remote Indigenous Schools', by Ilana Snyder and Denise Beale also specifically provides a demonstration of how a language policy to make English the instructional medium, itself a complex educational issue connected to the inter-communal politics between indigenous communities and settlers, affects other languages and speakers of other languages. Drawing upon work in the Northern Territory of Australia, they take us through the policy pronouncements and the political responses analyzing the value-laden understandings of language and literacy education that informed the initial policy. They look at the relationships between English and indigenous languages from a historical perspective and then track the current policy moves including a recent climb down and consider its implications. Like Prinsloo and other authors in this volume, they argue that the debates illustrate the deeply political and value-laden nature of language and language policy, in which questions of power, ideology and politics are central. They also address the literacy and assessment dimension of these perspectives, agreeing with the overall view in this volume that literacy tests and the apparatus of testing are never neutral. As in the South Africa case (see Chapter 2), whilst some children have the cultural and social capital that helps them to understand the particular language associated with testing and to decode the questions in language tests, for others, such as students in remote communities for whom English is often their second, third or fourth language, there are no such advantages. They track the history of these debates in Australia as a background to their analysis of the present situation, taking us through the various recent policy shifts regarding both language and literacy. In this, they draw upon authors in the theoretical literature such as Cummins (1999), Lo Bianco (2008a, 2008b) and May (1998, 2008) and conclude with a general, 'academic' argument that the policy shifts they identify took place without adequate understanding of such theoretical perspectives. In their conclusion they argue that the decisions they describe displayed a lack of understanding of the ways both language and literacy are acquired, which brings them back to the starting point of the chapter: the value-laden nature of language and literacy education.

Chapter 4, '(Re)Writing English: Putting English in Translation', by Bruce Horner and Min Lu challenges many of the assumptions in US composition classrooms that are so taken for granted that people are not aware of the need to be thinking in alternative ways. The authors present some of the criticisms and debates which show that some of the work in the fields of English as a Lingua Franca and World Englishes, which recognize the diversity within English today, reinforces the static view of the language (see Chapters 6 and 7 for a discussion on this issue in relation to school language and literacy and English language). The US, it seems, is a further case study for the gap between what research can tell us and what policy and educational institutions attempt to impose on language and literacy users. Their focus is on post-secondary writing instruction for 'L1' and 'L2' speakers of English in light of changes to our understanding of English as a medium. They take this approach because they claim that the powerful policy debates about ELF and World Englishes have in fact mostly been applied to the 'outer circle' and they want to argue here that many of the issues are also relevant to those in the 'inner circle' of the Anglo-American sphere. In fact, English as a uniform and static code, the mastery and preservation of which are linked indelibly to social identity and to individual, national and global economic well-being, is an ideology that dominates language instruction in the 'inner circle' too and whilst this persists it is likely to dominate language instruction outside that realm as well. They take as their case the field of composition studies in the US, where it is assumed that writing in the academy will take place in Standard English. Having already read similar accounts in South Africa and in Australia, the reader may well be prepared for some of the arguments put forward here, but the distinctive point made by Horner and Lu is that in the US it may appear more 'natural' to favor a 'standard' view of English. This ethnocentric view, however, then extends, with US influence, beyond the boundaries to other countries. Given such hegemony, it behooves us, they claim, to examine the implications of research destabilizing the universality, 'purity' and the fixed character of English as a medium for composition instruction in the US too. It might at first sight appear that at least some of the research on ELF and World Englishes has moved in this direction, but Horner and Lu argue that in fact, paradoxically, such scholarship appears to reinforce particular tenets of monolingual ideology. They want to replace this with what they call a 'translingual' approach to language. Such an approach treats all reading and writing as involving translation across languages, discourses and forms of language, and highlights the necessity of the contribution of writers' and readers' concrete labor to the production of meaning and the maintenance and transformation of specific language practices. Whilst working this argument through the specific character of composition studies in the US, they argue that such a discussion might also provoke the development of comparable pedagogies in other areas of language instruction concerned with 'English'. In that sense the particular debates about composition can be located in the wider issues raised by this volume concerning 'English as a medium of instruction'. They proceed with this account by first summarizing and locating scholarship on ELF and on World Englishes, which they see as demonstrating the ideological basis of the continuing power of 'English only' in language education. They want, instead, to move towards definitions of ELF that radically challenge the notions of language that such cores, and the attempts to identify them, represent. This perspective, then, would recognize diverse meanings and the necessity of the concrete labor of language users in the struggle over and production of meaning. What they term the 'archipelago' model and what Lea and Street (1998, 2006) have described as the 'academic socialization' perspective on academic literacies both, they claim, treat literacy as autonomous rather than ideological: operating autonomously on writers and readers to produce specific, determined effects. The Academic Literacies perspective, drawing on the ideological model of literacy, sees instead the agency of writers and readers exercised through their practices with literacy/ies, an approach that matches more closely the 'translanguaging' view being put forward by Horner and Lu in this Volume, Chapter 4. It is the ability to transform written forms that is crucial for learner development, a point they reinforce with an example of such transformative language use that would normally be seen simply as 'error'. Such close analysis of a student's writing, of the kind that is traditionally applied only to the work of canonical, published writers, can help the teacher to help the student challenge the dominant model of language and literacy and thereby rethink their experiences and beliefs. Rewriting English, then, rather than learning to write 'in' 'English', is an ongoing process, for both teachers and students, of learning and doing, of participating in language as living 'constitutive activity'.

Chapter 5, 'Multilingual and Multimodal Resources in Genre-based Pedagogical Approaches to L2 English Content Classrooms', by Angel Lin offers a historical overview of language policy in Hong Kong schools to demonstrate how such issues play out in real school contexts. The chapter also includes specific discussions of challenges associated with the change of the instructional medium and solutions for these challenges that would require loosening of language boundaries (see Chapter 4 for a related discussion). Lin locates these developments in English in Hong Kong in the larger context of original colonial influence and more recently global influences on language use, including science, technology, social media and the internet, for all of which English has become an indispensable linguistic resource. This leads to a range of dilemmas and difficulties associated with English-medium education in these contexts: Lin illustrates how this works out in the case of Hong Kong and suggests how introducing multilingualism, multimodalities and genre-based pedagogies into the L2 English content classroom might offer a way out of these dilemmas. One current policy dilemma in Hong Kong is how to ensure that students' proficiency in English can be improved, while avoiding the social and educational costs of the previous policy of linguistic streaming, an issue that we have seen worked through in different countries in other chapters of this volume (Chapters 2, 3 and 4). In order to break away from the static concept of languages as discrete monolithic entities, educators and policy-makers need think outside of the box where they might find a new space for the exploration of innovative means to achieve reachable goals in both English learning and content learning. Lin offers four directions that might offer potential for developing innovative ways out of such difficulties and dilemmas: (i) developing multiple flexible approaches to content-based L2 instruction; (ii) breaking away from the traditional immersion model for L2 English; (iii) drawing on multimodal and continua theories of langauge and communication; and (iv) drawing on genre-based multilingual, multimodal and popular cultural resources in program design. As with the other chapters, she locates these proposals in the larger theoretical context, notably: Hallidayan linguistic theory, particularly work on the language of science, which she illustrates with detailed examples; genre theory and how it has been used with respect to academic literacy, calling on US as well as Australian experiences; and theories of scaffolding and bridging in L2 contexts, drawing on relevant work in the ESL field, particularly Gibbons' (1993, 2002, 2008, 2009) extension of Cummins' analytic frame regarding Basic Interpersonal Communication Skills (BICS) and Cognitive Academic Language Proficiency (CALP). As with the other authors in this volume, she tests out these larger theoretical principles on specific case study data, in this case on accounts of the Integrated Science subject in junior secondary schools in Hong Kong. She sees this as a pilot model for future research in this area, both for other L2 English content subjects and more broadly in other L2 contexts. She concludes with a call for future research to explore and test out the effectiveness of different innovative multilingual and multimodal approaches to the provision of English academic literacy in the 'expanding circle' contexts, a call that is central to this volume as a whole as other authors have testified.

Chapter 6, 'Multimodal Literacies and Assessment: Uncharted Challenges in the English Classroom', by Heather Lotherington and Natalia Sinitskaya Ronda picks up the broadening of literacy theory to embrace multimodal literacies and sees this as being in direct conflict with the traditional view of literacy on which current patterns of assessment in educational contexts are based. In this case the authors' experience is in the Canadian province of Ontario where language and literacy share a curriculum for the duration of formal schooling, with a focus on *Language* in the elementary–junior years, and *English* in the secondary years. This, they say, in effect equates literacy to written English (in English-medium schools). They briefly describe how we got here – via the history of mass schooling in Canada and the newer global influence of English, which has somehow, in educational circles, not caught up with the complex range of communicative practices this now involves. Instead, English is defined in terms of the familiar narrow parameters of accuracy and fluency in language use. As the other authors have pointed out, with examples from a variety of international contexts, definitions of these parameters now require other dimensions to capture complementary and hybridized modes of expression, dynamic texts and participatory authorship structures. In the case of the English classrooms they describe here systemic change in language and literacy education has lagged sadly behind these new dimensions despite sporadic experiments, in Canada and other countries, of the kind other authors have described in this volume. Lotherington and Ronda expand on this with an account of new concepts of communication, notably digital communication, which they see as fluid, multimodal and increasingly less reliant on textual information. They draw on authors such as the New London Group, Tan and others who have both laid out the conceptual frame for such understanding and also considered its application to educational contexts and in particular to language and literacy classrooms. The authors themselves pick this up here as they provide concrete examples of their own experimental forays in multimodal literacies in the English classroom in the Ontario context, showing for instance how pupils in a grade 4/5 special education class engaged in complex, creative work that is not tapped in the limited standardized assessment vehicles used by the testing bodies. Drawing on this and other examples, they look to user engagement in social networking, fanfiction and interactive gaming sites, to name a few, to discover working models of how to engage and refashion educational content, and how to take a problem, work out and customize solutions. Against this, the dominant model in Canada and other countries remains focused on conventional use of grammar, spelling and sentence mechanics at an individual level. Lotherington and Ronda conclude by challenging this in their own national context and more broadly, and argue that in a communicative world where virtual basics and glocal learning communities are driving exciting new horizons in learning one thing is certain: we cannot continue to make judgments of this learning based on individual paper tests of standard English grammar and information retrieval from static documents (this resonates with the themes in Chapters 4 and 7).

Chapter 7, 'Beyond Labels and Categories in English Language Teaching: Critical Reflections on Popular Conceptualizations', by Martin Dewey provides a critical analysis of many of the prevailing assumptions in ELT through an examination of language labels widely used by teaching professional and researchers. In particular it touches upon the heterogeneity and 'messiness' of English as well as its political complexity, which are also addressed in other chapters. Like the other authors, Dewey argues that the concept of English itself, as both a subject and medium of education, is in need of considerable rethinking in light of the enormous contextual diversity surrounding the use of this language. He addresses this by subjecting current professional practices in ELT to some 'reflective thought', in particular through asking the question 'what counts as English?', especially in relation to the extent to which English has become a globally diffuse language, as we have seen in the examples provided through this volume. At this conceptual level, Dewey argues that the terms currently in favor, such as EFL (English as a Foreign Language), ESL (English as a Second Language), are heavily laden with traditional intellectual assumptions about language that do not adequately reflect current realities regarding the global sociolinguistics of English. He turns instead to the relatively new paradigm of ELF (English as a Lingua Franca), which marks a distinct attempt to rethink the way English is conceptualized (see Chapter 4 for a related discussion). In a way that readers will find helpful at this stage of the volume, Dewey takes us through the meanings that have developed in educational and testing circles for the key terms EFL and ESL, linking them to methodological and theoretical underpinnings. Agreeing with Leung (2005) for instance, he points out that a key underpinning concept, 'Communicative Language Teaching' (CLT), derived from the ethnography of communication of Del Hymes. The term 'communicative competence' has, in fact, been commandeered in the ELT field for a much narrower, more prescriptive meaning, based on idealized and projected universalisms. Shifts in the field, such as Tasked Based Learning, apparently away from such narrower conceptualizations have, in fact, inherited the same reductive notion of communication. The discourse has been almost exclusively concerned with discussion and development of approaches and methods, including both pedagogy and, on a large industrial scale, assessment, with the result that very little attention has been paid to addressing what exactly we mean when we talk about 'English' as a foreign/second/additional language. This is a question that the authors in the present volume have reviewed at length, in keeping with Dewey's own quest for deeper conceptual understanding that can lead to better and more effective pedagogy. After exploring these traditional concepts in some detail, Dewey concludes by arguing, like Canagarajah (1999), for the adoption of a multi-norm approach to English, where norms and standards that are found outside English as a Native Language contexts are applied whenever relevant. This approach is in line with the position taken in the other chapters as authors have called upon theories of multimodality, literacy as social practice (Chapters 4 and 5), translingualism, and so on. Dewey's own work, for instance, has begun to show how flexibility in the use of linguistic resources can enhance effectiveness and efficiency of communication. This, as he points out at the outset, entails a re-conceptualization of the terms used to describe English, which represents a challenge to the very nature of conceptual beliefs about what language itself is.

References

Canagarajah, A.S. (1999) *Resisting Linguistic Imperialism in English Teaching.* Oxford: Oxford University Press.

Cummins, J. (1999) Alternative paradigms in bilingual education research: Does theory have a place? *Educational Researcher* 28, 26–41.

Gibbons, P. (1993) *Learning to Learn in a Second Language.* Portsmouth, NH: Heinemann.

Gibbons, P. (2002) *Scaffolding Language, Scaffolding Learning: Teaching Second Language Learners in the Mainstream Classroom.* Portsmouth, NH: Heinemann.

Gibbons, P. (2008) 'It was taught good and I learned a lot': Intellectual practices and ESL learners in the middle years. *Australian Journal of Language and Literacy* 31 (2), 155–173.

Gibbons, P. (2009) *English Learners, Academic Literacy, and Thinking: Learning in the Challenge Zone.* Portsmouth, NH: Heinemann.

Halliday, M.A.K. (1973) *Explorations in the Functions of Language.* London: Edward Arnold.

Halliday, M.A.K. (1975) *Learning How to Mean: Explorations in the Development of Language.* London: Edward Arnold.

Halliday, M.A.K. and (revised by) Matthiessen, C.M.I.M. (2004) *An Introduction to Functional Grammar* (3rd edn). London: Arnold.

Hymes, D. (1972) On communicative competence. In J. B. Pride and J. Holmes (eds) *Sociolinguistics* (pp. 269–293). London: Penguin.

Hymes, D. (1977) *Foundations in Socio-linguistics: An Ethnographic Approach.* London: Tavistock Publications.

Hymes, D. (1994) Towards ethnographies of communication. In J. Maybin (ed.) *Language and Litercy in Social Practice* (pp. 11–22). Clevdon: Multilingual Matters, in association with Open University.

Lea, M. and Street, B. (1998) Student writing and faculty feedback in higher education: An academic literacies approach. *Studies in Higher Education*, 23 (2), 157–172.

Lea, M.R. and Street, B.V. (2006) The 'academic literacies' model: Theory and applications. *Theory into Practice*, 45(Fall) (4), 368–377.

Leung, C. (2005) Convivial communication: Recontextualizing communicative competence. *International Journal of Applied Linguistics* 15 (2), 119–144.

Lo Bianco, J. (2008a) Bilingual education and socio-political issues. In J. Cummins and D. Corson (eds) *Encyclopedia of Language and Education* (2nd edn. Vol. 5), *Bilingual Education* (pp. 35–50). Dordrecht, The Netherlands: Kluwer Academic Publishers.

Lo Bianco, J. (2008b) Language policy and education in Australia. In J. Cummins and D. Corson (eds) *Encyclopedia of Language and Education*, (2nd edn. Vol. 5), *Bilingual Education* (pp. 343–353). Dordrecht, The Netherlands: Kluwer Academic Publishers.

May, S. (1998) Language and education rights for Indigenous peoples. *Language, Culture and Curriculum* 11 (3), 272–296.

May, S. (2008) Bilingual/immersion education: What the research tells us. In J. Cummins and D. Corson (eds) *Encyclopedia of Language and Education* (2nd edn. Vol. 5), *Bilingual Education* (pp. 19–34). Dordrecht, The Netherlands: Kluwer Academic Publishers.

1 Introduction: English in the Curriculum – Norms and Practices

Constant Leung and Brian Street

Introduction

This book is concerned with English as a medium of curriculum com-munication, particularly in English as an Additional/Second Language (EAL) contexts. The spread of English in the world in the past 200 years, initially through British colonial expansion and through globalisation of business and industry in more recent times, has been accompanied by a huge demand for English Language Teaching (ELT) in a variety of contexts. EAL is taught and learned in many ways – as a subject in school, university and adult education settings in countries such as China and Brazil; as a language of instruction in English-medium education catering to speakers of other languages in places where English is an official language such as Singapore and Hong Kong and also in some international schools; as a language of schooling for linguistic minorities in countries such as Australia and the UK; and as a vehicular lan-guage in content-language integrated language teaching (generally referred to as CLIL) in some schools in Europe and elsewhere. All of this does not even include the vast number of students who travel to English-speaking countries for general and vocational education at all levels. According to Graddol (2006: 101) worldwide there are two billion (approximately) learners of EAL at the present time.

Given the scale and the international reach of this language teaching enterprise, it is important to ask how English has been characterised in the professional language teaching literature, and how far the established characterisation corresponds with the ways in which it is understood and used in contemporary contexts. These two questions are fundamentally related to a number of pedagogic issues such as the content, methodology and norms of teaching and assessment (see Nunan, 1991; Richards & Rodgers, 2001, for a discussion on the connections between teaching methodology and conceptualisation of language). In this introductory chapter we will look at the ways in which English language has been discussed in the professional literature with a view to exploring the possibilities for conceptual broadening. We will first focus on the emergence of the concept of communicative competence and how it has been a major influence on curriculum development and professional practice in ELT for the best part of the past 30 years. Next we will suggest that, in the light of our changing understanding of how language works and the diverse and dynamic ways in which English is being used as an additional language in the world, the notion of communicative competence, as understood in language teaching, should take greater account of a practice view of language use (instead of a norm-based view). By a practice view we are referring to an understanding that has emerged especially in ethnographic and sociological studies that addresses not only the form and content of languages but also the social meanings and uses associated with them.

Some of the developments in the related field of literacy studies are instructive here. Distinguishing between events and practices in the literacy field, Street (2000: 21) suggests that

the concept of literacy practices ... attempt[s] to handle the events and the patterns of activity around literacy but to *link* them to something broader of a cultural and social kind.

And part of that broadening involves attending to the fact that in a literacy event we have brought to it concepts, social models regarding what the nature of this practice is and that make it work and give it meaning.

In the sociological literature, the work of Bourdieu (1991, and also Bourdieu & Passeron, 1977) has been particularly significant in challenging narrow models of language and events and replacing them with a broader conception of social capital and practice. As Grenfell (2012: 67) notes, earlier theorists

defined the study of language in terms of its formal, structural properties. Even the Chomskyan revolution of the 1950s is predicated on the notion of an 'ideal' speaker and, thus perfect competence. For Bourdieu, this model is simply something that does not exist. Moreover, the consequent methodology that seeks to see sense and significance in terms of an 'internalist' reading of language itself basically overlooks all the contextual (social, cultural) components that give linguistic events their meaning.

At first glance it may seem that in making this appeal to a more socially and culturally oriented approach to language and literacy, we are adopting an unnecessarily large canvass. However, as the classroom vignette in this chapter will show in a moment, what goes on when teachers and students engage in talk and in reading and writing is not a simple matter of manual driven didactic transmission. Indeed, the ways in which they use English to 'do' teaching and learning are unavoidably situated in a wider context of social norms and practices, curriculum affordances and constraints, and institutionally induced relationships, and at the same time, all the participants in the classroom activities are themselves social actors investing in particular social and cultural choices.

In the final section we will explore the conceptual implications of a practice-oriented notion of communicative competence for understanding the multifaceted manifestations of English in classroom and curriculum contexts. This discussion will draw on research in a number of related fields such as English as a Foreign Language (EFL), English as a Lingua Franca (ELF), language education and literacy studies (including NLS – 'New Literacy Studies'). We will use EAL as a super-coordinating term to refer to English whenever the speaker/learner already has another language, but will defer to the relevant 'native' nomenclature such as EFL and ELF where appropriate, particularly in citations (see Dewey, Chapter 7 this volume, for a detailed discussion on diverse contexts of and labels for ELT).

Communication as Language

The focus on communication in ELT has been a relatively recent phenomenon. In the 1950s language teaching, particularly foreign language teaching, was predominantly concerned with grammar and lexis delivered through a variety of teaching methods, for example, grammar translation and the audio-lingual method. For reasons of focus and scope we will not be providing a discussion on the move away from grammar-oriented approaches (see Howatt & Widdowson, 2004: Chapter 19; Richards & Rodger, 2001, for a discussion). Suffice it to say that the limitations of the grammar-based approaches were increasingly discussed in the 1960s and 1970s, and the merits of more real life-oriented approaches received extensive attention in the language teaching literature during this period. Halliday (1973, 1975; also Halliday et al., 1964) and Hymes (1972, 1977, 1994) were among those whose work made a significant contribution to the shift from a grammar orientation. We will now provide a brief account of the influential work of Halliday and Hymes to provide a perspective on the intellectual sensibilities of the principles underlying ELT practice today. (For a synopsis of the key ideas that influenced this paradigm shift, see Canale & Swain, 1980a; Leung, 2010, for an account of the impact of sociolinguistics on language teaching.)

A key concept in the work of Halliday and his associates is function in language. By function is meant the relationship between meaning and language expression (of which grammar is a part), which 'reflects the fact that language has evolved in the service of particular human needs ... what is really significant is that this functional principle is carried over and built into the grammar, so that the internal organization of the grammar system is also functional in character' (Halliday, 1975: 16). Seen in this light, meaning-making underpins the ways in which (any) language as a system is developed. More importantly for this discussion, meaning-making shapes the ways in which language is used. For Halliday language use can be broadly understood as serving three functional purposes, referred to as meta-functions in the Hallidayan literature:

• ideational – this meta-function is concerned with the use of language as a means to talk about the world and about oneself; it is instantiated whenever a 'speaker expresses his experience of the phenomena of the external world, and of the internal world of his own consciousness' (Halliday, 1975: 17);
• interpersonal – individuals, through language expressions, can adopt a role or a position in relation to other participants, express their own values and views; so language is a means 'whereby the speaker participates in ... [a] speech situation' (Halliday, 1975: 17) and, at the same time, a means for entering into particular social relationships with others;
• textual – language is seen as an enabling means for 'creating text' (Halliday, 1975: 17); language is the linguistic means deployed by speakers and writers to form spoken and written texts to make meaning in context; vocabulary, grammar and discourse organisation are all part of the means to form a text (increasingly other semiotic means such as graphics and video are also seen as text-forming means, see Kress & van Leeuwen, 2001).

These three meta-functions are analytical constructs; in actual language use all three are co-present. For instance, verbs such as 'argue', 'contend', 'express', 'think' and 'say' could be used to represent the same speech event, but 'she argued ...' has a very different discourse value than 'she said ...'. The two different lexical choices (textual meta-function) represent two different descriptions of a self-same event (ideational meta-function) indicating two different speaker positions. From a language teaching point of view this functional view of language and language use offers a propositionally and socially nuanced way of thinking about teaching content in relation to matching teaching focus to learner needs (see Schleppegrell *et al.*, 2004, for an example of pedagogic application of this approach).

The work of Hymes on ethnography of speaking was also influential in the re-orientation of language teaching; indeed his work on the concept of communicative competence can be seen as a key influence on the development of Communicative Language Teaching (CLT). For Hymes, when a child learns to communicate through language they have to learn how to use words (in utterances) in socially appropriate ways. So, having a grasp of words and grammar rules will not suffice; there are social conventions of use. By observing the ways in which language is used methodically one can build up a picture of language practice. The actual ways in which language is used in context can be arrived at empirically by asking these questions:

Whether (and to what degree) something is formally **possible**;

Whether (and to what degree) something is **feasible** in virtue of the means of implementation available;

Whether (and to what degree) something is **appropriate** (adequate, happy, successful) in relation to a context in which it is used and evaluated;

Whether (and to what degree) something is in fact done, actually **performed**, and what its doing entails. (Hymes, 1972: 281, original emphasis)

These empirical questions are clearly relevant to language teachers interested in finding a way to understand what counts as appropriate language form in context of use. This approach to understanding language not just as a lexis-and-grammar system, but also as language practice in context, allows teachers to gain greater traction on issues regarding appropriate models of language use for teaching.

Transforming Communication to Communicative Language Teaching

This broadening of the concerns of language teaching to take account of the importance of the 'social' in language use provided an important impetus for the development of CLT within ELT. In a series of papers Canale and Swain (1980a, 1980b; also Canale, 1983, 1984, among others) put forward a theoretical framework for communicative competence for additional/second language teaching which comprises four component competences:

(1) grammatical competence – this component refers to 'knowledge of lexical items and of rules of morphology, syntax ... and phonology' (Canale & Swain, 1980b: 29);

(2) sociolinguistic competence – this component is concerned with '... the extent to which utterances are produced and understood appropriately in different ... contexts depending on contextual factors such as status of participants, purposes of interaction, and norms and conventions of interaction ...' (Canale, 1983: 7);

(3) discourse competence – this component addresses '[u]nity of a text ... achieved through cohesion in form and coherence in meaning. Cohesion deals with how utterances are linked structurally and facilitates interpretation of a text. For example, the use of ... pronouns, synonyms ... coherence refers to the relationship among the different meanings in a text, where these meanings may be literal meanings, communicative functions and attitudes' (Canale, 1983: 9);

(4) strategic competence – this component attends to '... verbal and nonverbal communication strategies that may be called into action to compensate for breakdowns in communication due to performance variables or to insufficient competence [grammatical and/or sociolinguistic]' (Canale & Swain, 1980b: 30), and speaker actions that can '... enhance effectiveness of communication (e.g. deliberately slow or soft speech for rhetorical effect)' (Canale, 1983: 11).

It can be readily seen that there are traces of Halliday's and Hymes' work in this formulation of communicative competence. The influence of the concept of communicative competence has not dimmed in 30 years. It would be no exaggeration to say that it has set the parameters for curriculum and pedagogic discussions in language education worldwide. For instance, the politically and institutionally influential Common European Framework for Reference for Languages (CEFR) (Council of Europe, 2001) – a set of outcomes specifications designed to inform curriculum and assessment development – claims to be built on the concept of communicative competence. ELT, as pointed out earlier, continues to refer to communicative competence as its conceptual bedrock for CLT. Commercially produced textbooks, for instance, often make explicit claims of lineage to communicative competence; for example, Kay and Jones (2009) and Oxenden and Latham-Koenig (2006) link their contents to specific levels of proficiency specified in the CEFR.

There is, however, a difference between the conceptually and analytically oriented discussions on the social dimensions of language and language use, and the ways in which they have been rendered as principles in language teaching. The conceptual insight that there is an intimate connection between socially situated meaning and language form (e.g. Halliday), and the research imperative that communicative competence is to be established empirically through ethnographic observations (e.g. Hymes) have been re-contextualised as teaching (and learning) how to do things with language using 'appropriate' forms of language, implicitly normed on what native-speakers would say. Modal verbs such as 'would' and 'could', for example, are often presented as appropriate choices for polite expressions, pedagogically this kind of information is interwoven into teaching and learning activities. For instance, Brown's (2001: 43) formulation of CLT includes using classroom teaching techniques and learning activities 'to engage learners in the pragmatic, authentic, functional use of language for meaningful purposes', and making the teacher 'a facilitator and guide . . .' and '[s]tudents are therefore encouraged to construct meaning through genuine linguistics interaction with others'. Over time the 'pragmatic, authentic, functional use of language' has come to be interpreted in terms of what is likely to be said and done in idealised (and imagined) native English-speaking scenarios; in a fundamental sense the notion of language practice has morphed into pedagogic prescriptions (see Horner & Lu, Chapter 4 this volume, for a wider discussion). Perhaps the demands for 'teachable knowledge' in conventionally teacher-led pedagogy cannot easily accommodate the more research-oriented impulse that was embedded in the pioneering discussions on communicative competence. The need for a body of stable and usable samples of language in teaching is, in all probability, incompatible with a research sensibility that treats knowledge as provisional. In one way or another, communicative competence in ELT has come to be understood in terms of learners' capacity to reproduce what putative native-speakers would say in any given projected scenario (Leung, 2005). (For a wider discussion on native-speakerness, see Leung *et al.*, 1997.)

Literacy: From Skills to Practices

Both Hymes and Halliday made use of the concept of practice in putting forward social and functional views of language use and it was this in particular that those researching literacy in this period highlighted. The term itself has been defined in a straightforward way as the 'social uses and meanings of reading and writing' (Street, 1984: 1), avoiding the more loaded and contentious meanings evident in, for instance, national and international policy documents, such as the UK Literacy Strategy focus on letters and phonics (Goodwyn, 2011) or UNESCO's shifting definitions from function to skills in communicative technology (c.f. UNESCO, 2006). For researchers in what Gee (1990) and Street (1993) have referred to as 'New Literacy Studies', there was a basic problem with both the conceptualisation and pedagogy associated with such models of literacy that were dominant in both the academic and the educational policy circles until the 1990s (and still frequently invoked even today). Such models tended precisely to ignore the social dimension that we have been reviewing here. Instead, as Street (1984) argues, the model of literacy put forward assumed that reading and writing were somehow 'autonomous' of social practice. In this view, people would learn literacy first, including the formal features of grammar, lexis, orthography and phoneme/grapheme relations and after that they could apply their literacy to whatever texts and contexts were of interest. However, a social practice perspective sees the very act of acquiring literacy as itself social, and the definition of what counts as literacy in different contexts – including notably educational contexts – as not neutral but, as Street terms it, 'ideological'. The ideological model of literacy sees the acquisition and use of literacy practices as always embedded in social contexts and in social judgements of use and value. (For a further discussion see Street 1993.)

To research and understand how this happens, researchers have evolved a distinction between literacy events and literacy practices. Shirley Brice Heath (1983: 50) characterised a 'literacy event' as 'any occasion in which a piece of writing is integral to the nature of the participants' interactions and their interpretative processes'. Street (1984: 1) employed the phrase 'literacy practices' as a means of focussing upon 'the social practices and conceptions of reading and writing', although he later elaborated the term both to take account of 'events' in Heath's sense and to give greater emphasis to the social models of literacy that participants bring to bear upon those events and that give meaning to them (Street, 1988). David Barton, Mary Hamilton and colleagues at Lancaster University have taken up these concepts and applied them to their own research in ways that have been hugely influential both in the UK and internationally (e.g. Barton et al., 1999).

The concept of literacy practices, then, attempts to handle the events and the patterns of activity around literacy but to *link* them to something broader of a cultural and social kind. And part of that broadening involves attending to the fact that in a literacy event we have – often implicitly, in 'hidden' ways – brought to it concepts, social models regarding what the nature of this practice is and that make it work and give it meaning. Those models we cannot get at simply by sitting on the wall with a video camera and watching what is happening: you can video-capture literacy events but you cannot record literacy practices this way. There is an ethnographic issue here: we have to start talking to people, listening to them and linking their immediate experience to other things that they do as well. That is why it is often meaningless to just ask people about literacy as if it held the same meaning for everyone, as has been done in recent surveys (National Centre for Social Research, 1997; OECD, 1995). This is because what might give *meaning* to literacy events may actually be something that is not, in the first instance, thought of in terms of literacy at all. For instance, in the case of academic practices it may be about social relations and the academy in which the expectations of tutors in different disciplines, or the requirements on courses made by administrative committees, determine what counts, even whilst students are being told that 'academic literacy' involves general skills autonomous of context, discipline, and so on. For example, Lea and Street (1997) found that tutors were writing comments in the margins of students' essays, such as 'structure' and 'argument', but the students, as they moved across different tutors and courses, were finding that these terms had different meanings in different disciplines. Likewise, an administrative committee in one institution decided that feedback on student essays was taking too much academic time, so ruled that only one feedback sheet would be available at the end of the course – students were throwing these sheets away because they recognised that next term they would have different tutors for whom this feedback might not be relevant. Heath and McLaughlin (1993) found when discussing newspaper reading with urban adolescents in the USA that much of their activity did not count in their minds as literacy at all, so a superficial survey would have missed the significance of their actual literacy practices and perhaps labelled them non-readers, or more insultingly 'illiterate' as in much press coverage of this area. A recent book by Nabi *et al.* (2009) on literacy practices in Pakistan, appropriately titled *Hidden Literacies*, found several respondents who said, when asked about some piece of reading and writing that they were doing, 'This is not literacy.' One cannot, then, predict beforehand what will give meaning to a literacy event and what will link a set of literacy events to literacy practices. The concept of literacy practices, then, refers to this broader cultural conception of particular ways of thinking about and doing reading and writing in cultural contexts. One of the key issues, at both a methodological and a pedagogical level, is how can we characterise the shift from observing literacy events to conceptualising literacy practices. Much contemporary curriculum in literacy, and indeed in additional/second language education more generally, tends to provide formalised and de-contextualised models for student learning that focus upon particular events, usually narrowly determined by classroom requirements, but thereby miss the significance of social practices in giving meaning to what is being learned. A broader socially based pedagogy would help students see the 'hidden' features of language and literacy (cf. Street, 2009) and the ways in which they are learning to enact them, addressing the social functions as Halliday would say and the appropriate social meanings as Hymes would say. This applies as much to the learning of English language in general as to the learning of literacy in particular. The way to take account of the actual practices is an aspect of such learning that we believe needs special attention. An example of how this approach can help us 'see' aspects of classroom practice and the literacy involved, that might otherwise remain 'hidden', can be illustrated in the following account of a London classroom recently studied by the authors.[1]

A Classroom Vignette: English in Practice

In many of the classes that we observed in this ethnolinguistically diverse London school, there was a complex mix of modes of information – written, spoken, visual – configured in different locations – on the walls, in notebooks, on black/whiteboards – involving different technologies and formats – computer and internet sources displayed on a screen, textbooks, students' notebooks, posters, folders, cards for writing on. One other frequently observed feature was that the teachers often mentioned examination requirements as part of the lesson objectives. What we are offering here is a theoretically interested descriptive account of classroom activities with a view to foregrounding the 'practice' perspective.

In this Advanced Subsidiary level History class (17-year-olds, pre-university) students from a number of different language backgrounds were

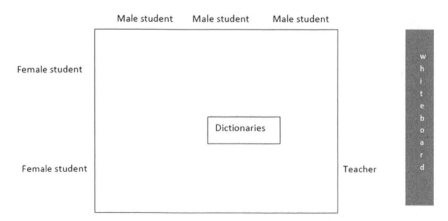

Figure 1.1 Classroom plan

engaged with work on the topic of 'The origins of the equal rights movement for women.' The teacher Donna took the students through a series of data sources and activities. The data sources included a PowerPoint presentation with five slides on the day's topic and homework, two handouts, 21 information cards and a poster. There were seven students, four boys, three girls (all with headscarves); three of the students were using EAL (see Figure 1.1). As they came into the room they chatted away in a lively style amongst themselves and with the teacher. The walls were full of writing and images.

The segment of the lesson reported here begins after the class had settled down and the teacher had announced the start of her teaching by drawing attention to the PowerPoint slide on the whiteboard. Pseudonyms are used for all participants in this vignette.

At the start of the lesson the teacher, Donna, draws the students' attention to the information on a slide displayed on the whiteboard (see Figure 1.2). The topic of the lesson is: The origins of the equal rights movement for women.

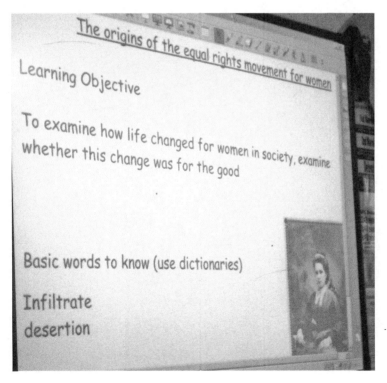

Figure 1.2 Slide 1

After introducing the topic the teacher asks the students to copy the information on the slide into their notebooks and to look up the meanings of the words 'infiltrate' and 'desertion' in the dictionary, a number of which have been placed on the table in front of the students. The students proceed with the copying task quietly; the teacher sits with the students and occasionally reminds them to use the dictionary.

After five minutes the teacher stands up and introduces a set of keywords on a new slide (see Figure 1.3).

The teacher tells the class that the main concept for the lesson is 'how life changed for women', and that the 'basic keywords' for this topic are on the left-hand side of the whiteboard. The students are asked to find a matching definition for each of the keywords from the right-hand side of the whiteboard. The teacher asks the students to write the words down on the board.

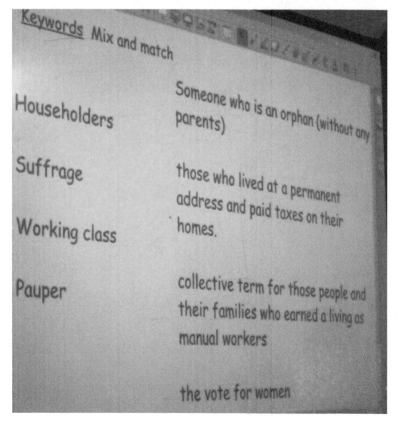

Figure 1.3 Slide 2

Classroom Talk Data Extract 1

(.) = short pause
(text) = uncertain transcription
(unclear) = unclear recording, cannot be transcribed
text = participants reading from book or document
⸮ = question/invitation
[added description, not transcription]
[sound such as laughter]
[= overlapping talk

```
01   Teacher:   these are words that you are going to be needing
02              to know throughout this lesson and not just in this
03              lesson but in next lesson and the lessons after (.)
04              okay so can you mix and match the definitions for me
05              please write them down [to one student] because
06              you need to know them (.) You need to them OK (.) and
07              if you don't know just leave gap and then we can come
08              back to it we can ask someone who does know (2) but I
09              want you to use your skill of deduction to work out
10              whether (.) you can find out the right answer OK (.)
11              without having any previous knowledge (.)think about
12              what (unclear) you think it could be
```

After the students have been working quietly on their own for about three minutes the teacher then nominates individual students to go up to the whiteboard to do a word-definition match.

Classroom Talk Data Extract 2

```
13   Teacher:   Nadifa can you come up here please?
14              [student goes to board]
15              can you match up householders for me please?
16              thank you very much [teacher handing a pen to N]
17              what is the definition of householders?
18              [student draws a line to link up 'householders' and its
19              definition, returns to her seat without speaking]
20   Teacher:   what is the definition of householders?
21              [reading from board]those who lived at a permanent
22              address (.) the word permanent is important here (.)
23              and paid taxes on their homes (.) OK (.) that is
24              going to become more and more important the more
25              we look at this topic area because householders
```

```
26              were the people generally the ones who [can] only
27              vote ...
```

The teacher nominates two other students to come up to the white-board to perform this matching exercise. The nominated students perform this task without speaking. After that the teacher completes the matching task for the last of the keywords, 'pauper', herself. But the teacher inter-sperses the board work with recall questions related to a focal keyword to the whole group. For instance, in relation to the last keyword, 'pauper', the teacher refers to the meanings of 'pauper' that she has discussed in previous classes:

Classroom Talk Data Extract 3

```
28   Teacher:   and the final one okay a pauper like in a pauper
29              apprentice (.) a pauper apprentice (.) remember
30              You did that in Year 9 History (.) you should
31              have (.) I taught you in Year 9 History (.)
32              OK right so a pauper apprentice is someone
33              who was made to work for nothing (.) but
34              usually paupers lived in a place called work
35              house (.) Year 9 History (.) what is a workhouse?
36   Jim:       where children go to work for nothing
37   Teacher:   or not just  children (.) anyone (though)
38   Jim:       work for nothing because they had nothing no job they
39              had no money
40   Teacher:   OK
```

At the end of this three-minute activity the whiteboard display is as shown in Figure 1.4.

The teacher now switches to next slide and a new focus: Women Today (see Figure 1.5). The teacher divides the students into small groups to discuss the issues on the whiteboard – one pair on 'work', another pair on 'marriage and divorce', and a group of three on 'education and sexuality'. The students are given one minute to do this. The students immediately engage in ani-mated talk. At the end of the allowed time the teacher tells the class to come back together and initiates a whole-class discussion.

Classroom Talk Data Extract 4

```
41   Teacher:   I'll start with start with marriage and divorce (.)
42              can you give me some of your opinions on what women
43              have today from marriage and divorce
```

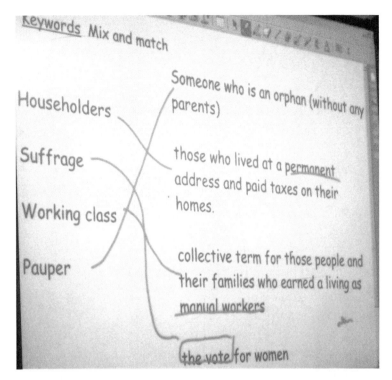

Figure 1.4 Slide 3

```
44   Nasreen:    it's exactly the same as men
45   Teacher:    so it's equal yeah
46   Nasreen:    and like they keep their own property and have
47               contracts for (.) (divorce) [and
48   Teacher:                                 [so they can file for
49               divorce and it is fully equal in in our society (.)
50               who tends to get control of children?
51   Students:   women
52   Teacher:    women OK yeah that's an interesting thing we're going
53               to come back to later on (.) OK so that's the thing
54               so in in law there's true equality in law in marriage
55               so that's the thing so in in law (.) what about err
56               things like things like err marital rape (.) is
57               that allowed?
58   Nasreen:    no (.) stopped in 1994
59   Teacher:    good stopped in 94 (.) what about beating up your
60               wife or your husband
```

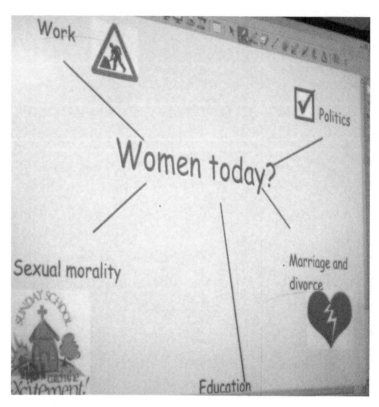

Figure 1.5 Slide 4

```
61  Nasreen:  that's abuse you can't do that
62  Teacher:  can't do that (2) what erm what about having an
63            affair?
64  Nasreen:  that's alright
65  Emran:    that's a moral issue
66            [student laughters, simultaneous animated talk]
67  Nasreen:  normally it's alright (.) [so in a legal way
68  Teacher:                            [so so so (.) legality wise
69            it's OK for who who (.) the man or the woman?
70            [simultaneous student talk]
71  Nasreen:  there's nothing wrong with it like
72  Emran:    it's a moral issue (.) it's not a legal issue
73  Teacher:  OK so for instance  (.) so is is it (.) in that sense
74            (.) what I'm asking you is is it for just men or for
75            women?
```

76   Students: [*several voices*] both
77   Teacher: both (.) that's what I am trying to get across (.) so
78   it's equal OK (.) what about work then?

In total this segment is approximately 9–10 minutes (of a 60 minute lesson). There is constant interweaving between different 'modes' of language (talk, writing, reading, listening) and literacy activities, involving a variety of multimodal material use. The lesson started with little or no spoken introduction into the topic; students had to copy keywords displayed on the whiteboard and then use a dictionary to find out the word meanings for themselves. The nature of social participation shifted rapidly within minutes and often rested upon implicit rules and routines, for example, concept (word) and definition (word strings) matching activities that included students performing at the whiteboard. In terms of the knowledge and the time frames being invoked, the past and the present constantly ran into each other as the teacher referred, for instance, to earlier voting rights and to contemporary laws regarding marriage and divorce, and she also referred to earlier lessons, as in Extract 4 regarding her explanations of the word 'pauper'.

The lesson moved at a very fast pace – the teacher moved from one slide to the next slide, asked questions, then instigated a discussion around key terms. There were rapid transitions between teacher-led discussion and short question and answer sessions; at the same time there was considerable student–student talk. Other activities in this lesson (not in the vignette reported here) involved students writing in their notebooks, often associated with looking at visual images and looking up words in dictionaries. Links between all of these activities were established via keywords, teacher questions and students' hands-on activities – writing, matching and gluing word strips together. In the latter case, the shifts between modes and the use of material artefacts (cf. Pahl & Rowsell, 2010) involved reading short word strings from cards, selecting appropriate ones, then sticking them on to posters, which were then placed in their folders.

As researchers interested in both language and literacy practices, particularly as they relate to students from EAL backgrounds, our interest was guided by the conceptual frames indicated earlier – notably NLS and EAL learning from communicative perspectives. From the perspective of NLS, we might say that we can observe all of the events described here, but recognise that this is not enough, we also need to ask how the students and their teacher – and the researchers – made sense of them. In order to understand 'what's going on' here, we needed, as we noted above, to make the shift from events to practices, to begin to identify the meanings and concepts underlying the events and their location in social and institutional contexts. What social, cultural and ideological components were working here to construct meanings? For instance, the Academic Literacies research asks us to focus on the different genres, practices and social interactions involved in students engaging with formal requirements (Lea & Street, 1997, 2006). We might ask, in relation to the data above, how did the students make links between the different sources of information, the different kinds of task, the words highlighted and the larger spoken and written accounts required? A key issue was how such activity and use of data sources linked with the examination tasks required, such as particular written genres. How were students learning the different genres of writing required for examination and how did their 'ordinary' language usage relate to that required for these tasks? The more recent work on multimodality (e.g. Kress, 2000; Kress *et al.*, 2005; Lotherington & Ronda, Chapter 6, this volume) asks us to identify the meanings associated with different modes and different artefacts. As the students moved from reading words on the whiteboard to talking about them, and writing them into notebooks and folders, what contribution did the artefacts and the ways in which they were used make to the overall meaning-making? At the same time, EAL literature draws attention to the varieties of English being called upon in these specific academic tasks, including how they may differ from those that students are familiar with in everyday communication. The data above, for instance, provides rich and complex examples of the focus on content vocabulary and of the academic discourse the teacher is calling upon. From the point of view of the implicit interpersonal relationship embedded in the teacher talk, demonstrative utterances such as 'these are words that you are going to be needing ...' (line 1, Classroom Talk Data Extract 1) and nominated requests such as 'Nadifa can you come up here please?' (line 13, Classroom Talk Data Extract 2) signal an assumed power position on the part of the teacher. In terms of subject content words such as 'pauper', not frequently encountered in everyday English today, were highlighted by the teacher and then associated with epithets used in specific legalistic and administrative frameworks, such as 'apprentice'. And yet this focus on subject-specific meanings and their language expressions was interspersed with talk concerned with classroom organisation and task management. English is both a constituent and an embodiment of such a flight of multifaceted meaning-making Here we see subject-related vocabulary, what Halliday might refer to as 'register', and everyday language expressions interwoven in a way that Hymes might term 'appropriate' by virtue of the fact that this communicative event happened.

A practice view would allow us to see that English is considerably more complex and intricate than any prescriptive model would allow. English, in this case English in an educational context, is, among other things, the inter-weaving of everyday expressions and specialist register, such as 'academic English', uses of different sources of information embodied in different mate-rialities and hands-on activities, and language resourcing in a broader sense (see Prinsloo, Chapter 2 and Snyder & Beale, Chapter 3). Above all, the con-tent of the subject can be seen as a core meaning from which the various activities are developed, and to which they owe their pedagogic coherence in context (see Lin, Chapter 5, this volume). The vignette presented in this dis-cussion provides a glimpse of the potential yield of looking at English as part of social and language practice. Taken as a whole, the chapters in the volume provide a theoretically informed and 'practice' minded discussion that can help us build a rich and more complex picture than the more norm-driven language and literacy approaches that have dominated both research and pedagogy in English.

Note

(1) Data extracts shown in this discussion are drawn from the research project: Modelling for Diversity: Academic Language and Literacies in School and University, ESRC-funded – RES-062-23-1666 (2009–2011). Researchers: Constant Leung and Brian Street.

References

Barton, D., Hamilton, M. and Ivanič, R. (eds) (1999) *Situated Literacies: Reading and Writing in Context*. London: Taylor and Francis.

Bourdieu, P. (1991) *Language and Symbolic Power*. London: Polity Press.

Bourdieu, P. and Passeron, J. (1977) *Reproduction in Education, Society and Culture*. Beverley Hills, CA: Sage.

Brown, H.D. (2000) *Principles of Language Learning and Teaching* (4th edn). White Plains, NY: Pearson Education (Longman).

Canale, M. (1983) From communicative competence to language pedagogy. In J. Richards and J. Schmidt (eds) *Language and Communication* (pp. 2–27). London: Longman.

Canale, M. (1984) A communicative approach to language proficiency assessment in a minority setting. In C. Rivera (ed.) *Communicative Competence Approaches to Language Proficiency Assessment: Research and Application* (pp. 107–122). Clevedon: Multilingual Matters.

Canale, M. and Swain, M. (1980a) *A Domain Description for Core FSL: Communication Skills*. Ontario: Ministry of Education.

Canale, M. and Swain, M. (1980b) Theoretical bases of communicative approaches to second language teaching and testing. *Applied Linguistics* 1 (1), 1–47.

Council of Europe. (2001) *Common European Framework of Reference for Languages: Learning, Teaching, Assessment*. Cambridge: Cambridge University Press.

Gee, J.P. (1990) *Social Linguistics and Literacies: Ideology in Discourse*. London and Philadelphia: Falmer Press.

Goodwyn, A. (ed.) (2011) *The Literacy Project: A Critical Response to the Literacy Strategy and the Framework for English*. London: Routledge.

Graddol, D. (2006) *English Next*. London: British Council.

Grenfell, M. (2012) Bourdieu, languge, and education. In M. Grenfell, D. Bloome, C. Hardy, K. Pahl, R. J. and B. Street (eds) *Langugage, Ethnography, and Education: Bridging New Literacy Studies and Bourdieu* (pp. 50–70). New York: Routledge.

Halliday, M.A.K. (1973) *Explorations in the Functions of Language*. London: Edward Arnold.

Halliday, M.A.K. (1975) *Learning How to Mean: Explorations in the Development of Language*. London: Edward Arnold.

Halliday, M.A.K., McIntosh, A. and Strevens, P. (1964) *The Linguistic Sciences and Language Teaching*. London: Longman.

Heath, S.B. (1983) *Ways With Words: Language, Life and Work in Communities and Classrooms*. New York: Cambridge University Press.

Heath, S.B. and McLaughlin, M. (1993) *Identity and Inner-City Youth: Beyond Ethnicity and Gender*. New York: Teachers College Press.

Howatt, A.P.R. and Widdowson, H.G. (2004) *A History of English Language Teaching* (2nd edn). Oxford: Oxford University Press.

Hymes, D. (1972) On communicative competence. In J.B. Pride and J. Holmes (eds) *Sociolinguistics* (pp. 269–293). London: Penguin.

Hymes, D. (1977) *Foundations in Socio-linguistics: An Ethnographic Approach*. London: Tavistock Publications.

Hymes, D. (1994) Towards ethnographies of communication. In J. Maybin (ed.) *Language and Litercy in Social Practice* (pp. 11–22). Clevedon: Multilingual Matters, in association with Open University.

Kay, S. and Jones, V. (2009) *New Inside Out*. Oxford: MacMillan.

Kress, G. (2000) Multimodality. In B. Cope and M. Kalantzis (eds) *Multiliteracies: Literacy Learning and the Design of Social Futures* (pp. 182–202). London: Routledge.

Kress, G. and van Leeuwen, T. (2001) *Multimodal Discourse: The Modes and Media of Contemporary Communication*. London: Arnold.

Kress, G., Jewitt, K., Bourne, J., Frank, A., Hardcastle, A., Jones, J. and Read, E. (2005) *English in Urban Classrooms: A Multimodal Perspective on Teaching and Learning*. New York: Routledge.

Lea, M. and Street, B. (1997) Student writing and faculty feedback in higher education: An academic literacies approach. *Studies in Higher Education* 23 (2), 157–172.

Lea, M.R. and Street, B.V. (2006) The 'academic literacies' model: Theory and applications. *Theory into Practice* 45 Fall (4), 368–377.

Leung, C. (2005) Convivial communication: Recontextualizing communicative competence. *International Journal of Applied Linguistics* 15 (2), 119–144.

Leung, C. (2010) Language teaching and language assessment. In R. Wodak, B. Johnstone and P. Kerswill (eds) *The Sage Handbook of Socio-linguistics* (pp. 545–564). London: Sage.

Leung, C., Harris, R. and Rampton, B. (1997) The idealised native speaker, reified ethnicities, and classroom realities. *TESOL Quarterly* 31 (3), 543–560.

Nabi, R., Rogers, A. and Street, B. (2009) *Hidden Literacies: Ethnographic Studies of Literacy and Numeracy Practices in Pakistan*. Uppingham: Uppingham Press.

National Centre for Social Research. (1997) *British Social Attitudes Survey*. Colchester, Essex: UK Data Archive.

Nunan, D. (1991) *Language Teaching Methodology: A Textbook for Teachers*. New York: Prenticehall.

OECD (1995) *OECD Education Statistics 1985–92*. Paris: Organisation for Economic Co-operation and Development.

Oxenden, C. and Latham-Koenig, C. (2006) *New English File*. Oxford: Oxford University Press.

Pahl, K. and Rowsell, J. (2010) *Artifactual Literacies: Every Object Tells a Story*. Columbia University, New York: Teachers College Press.

Richards, J.C. and Rodgers, T.S. (2001) *Approaches and Methods in Language Teaching* (2nd edn). Cambridge: Cambridge University Press.

Schleppegrell, M.J., Achugar, M. and Orteíza, T. (2004) The grammar of history: Enhancing content-based instruction through a functional focus on language. *TESOL Quarterly* 38 (1), 67–93.

Street, B. (1984) *Literacy in Theory and Practice*. Cambridge: Cambridge University Press.

Street, B. (1988) Literacy practices and literacy myths. In R. Saljo (ed.) *The Written Word: Studies in Literate Thought and Action* (pp. 59–72). Heidelberg: Springer-Verlag Press.

Street, B. (ed.) (1993) *Cross-Cultural Approaches to Literacy*. Cambridge: Cambridge University Press.

Street, B. (2000) Literacy events and literacy practices. In M. Martin-Jones and K. Jones (eds) *Multilingual Literacies: Comparative Perspectives on Research and Practice* (pp. 17–29). Amsterdam: John Benjamin's.

Street, B. (2009) Hidden features of academic paper writing. *Working Papers in Educational Linguistics, UPenn* 24 (1), 1–17.

UNESCO (2006) *EFA Global Monitoring Report 2006: Literacy for Life*. Geneva: UNESCO. http://unesdoc.unesco.org/images/0014/001416/141639e.pdf. Accessed 17th April 2012.

2 What Counts as English?

Mastin Prinsloo

There is something going on when policy statements from national government and the Education Ministry set out one policy direction for language
in education and practice takes a different direction. This chapter examines
the divergences between what educational policy calls for in South African
schools with regard to language and learning and what takes place in schools.
Drawing on an examination of language policy statements in South Africa
and on school-based ethnographic data I develop an analysis that starts to
account for the difference between language policy imperatives and schooling practices.[1]

I suggest that South African education policy is a good example of how
constructs to do with language in education policy rely on familiar but problematic ideas about language, development and nation building. The post-
apartheid South African Constitution and ensuing policy statements from
the Education Ministry employ an idea of languages as autonomous, boundaried entities and combine this understanding of languages with discourses
on language rights and of language endangerment. However, evidence of
language practices in schools and in the wider society suggests both a popular disregard for, as well as an institutional ambiguity over, these ideas about
boundaried languages and language endangerment/protection.

I draw on interactional sociolinguistic and ethnographic research
(Blommaert, 2005; Heller, 2007; Makoni & Pennycook, 1997) that has raised
questions about current policy formulations of language and argue that
South African policy for schooling provides a good example of the sorts of
problems that follow the use of popularised but essentialised and reified
constructs of language. That research variously suggests that these constructs of language have social origins, and specifically European origins,
from 19th-century nationalist movements that linked 'a language' to 'a
nation' and then defended that language through political means. The contrasting perspective developed in interactional sociolinguistics is that users
draw on linguistic resources that are organised in ways that make sense

under specific conditions (Heller, 2007: 1). This approach studies language as situated social practice. From this perspective the term 'English', or any other named language, is misleading shorthand for a diverse range of language varieties, genres, registers and practices. Such resources are not equally distributed amongst users of these resources and they carry different social weightings or valuations. A social practices perspective starts from the assumption that what counts about language and literacy is how it is done: what one does with it (Austin, 1975; Duranti, 2010; Gumperz & Hymes, 1972; Street, 1984). There are different ways of doing language and of linking (sometimes new) language forms to culturally meaningful and socially significant practices, in stratified social conditions where language resources carry social value for reasons that are not simply to do with their functionality (Bourdieu, 1991).

In the policy statements that I first examine here there are numerous examples of a conception of language as an autonomous object in its own right, monolithic and homogeneous, where languages are conceived as systems rather than practices. I start with a typical example from policy statements of how an idea of language is summoned and then endorsed: the introduction to the *Language Policy for Higher Education* statement produced by the South African Ministry of Education in 2002 describes South Africa as 'a country of many languages and tongues' but notes that these have not always been 'working together'.

> In the past, the richness of our linguistic diversity was used as an instrument of control, oppression and exploitation. The existence of different languages was recognised and perversely celebrated to legitimise the policy of 'separate development' that formed the cornerstone of apartheid. However, in practice, all our languages were not accorded equal status. The policy of 'separate development' resulted in the privileging of English and Afrikaans as the official languages of the apartheid state and the marginalisation and under-development of African and other languages. (Ministry of Education, 2002: 1)

The policy statement goes on to point out that

> the use of language policy as an instrument of control, oppression and exploitation was one of the factors that triggered the two great political struggles that defined South Africa in the twentieth century – the struggle of the Afrikaners against British imperialism and the struggle of the black community against white rule. Indeed, it was the attempt by the apartheid state to impose Afrikaans as a medium of instruction in black

schools that gave rise to the mass struggles of the late 1970s and 1980s. (Ministry of Education, 2002: 1–2)

The statement proceeds to identify a 'role for all our languages working together to build a common sense of nationhood' that is consistent with the values of 'democracy, social justice and fundamental rights', which are enshrined in the Constitution. The statement therefore endorses the recognition by apartheid ideologues of the distinct characters of separate languages, tongues and groups but accuses them of perversely entrenching those distinctions under laws of separation, rather than celebrating diversity. The view of language is the same, then, for both apartheid and post-apartheid policies – in both cases languages are frozen in time, and the discourse foregrounds the languages themselves and sidelines the actual users of these language resources. In reality, of course, it is the language users who interact, struggle, compete, dominate and cooperate with each other, rather than the languages. It would not be such a problem to present social struggle in this way if the languages did effectively stand for distinct groups of people whose group identities and languages emerged straightforwardly from the past and proceeded unproblematically into the future, but this is, of course, not the case. This approach also avoids the difficult issue of what the contrasting contemporary reach, scope and scale of operations of these several languages are, perhaps because, like elsewhere in Africa, these questions of scale follow historical (colonial) tracks, where the language of status is an ex-colonial language. Insisting on parity amongst 11 rather arbitrarily drawn sets of linguistic resources does not change the fact that there are linguistic hierarchies operating, here and everywhere else. The assumptions around boundedness, authenticity and language equality are ideological, in that they erase linguistic complexities and assume linguistic homogeneity where there is diversity. The strategy for equalising the designated languages works on the assumption that language operates normally as a neutral social medium, and that directed social planning can 'level the playing fields', whereas sociolinguistic research shows that language always operates as a non-neutral medium in stratified social contexts of all kinds (Bourdieu, 1991; Duranti, 2010). These inequalities operate just as much within designated languages, in terms of the varieties and their uses within that language, as across them.

The problem with these language policy statements starts with the Constitution. The Constitution of the Republic of South Africa sets out the case for the equal status of the languages of South Africa. In its opening chapter, under the heading 'Founding Provisions' the Constitution first names the 11 'official languages of the Republic'[2] (Constitution of South Africa, SA Govt Act 108 of 1996, clause 6.1). Second, noting the 'historically diminished use and status of the indigenous languages of our people', the Constitution stipulates that 'the state must take practical and positive measures to elevate the status and advance the use of these languages' (clause 6.2). The same section of the Constitution goes on to set out areas of flexibility that the government has regarding local use of selected official languages, but insists that 'languages must enjoy parity of esteem and must be treated equitably'. It is quite clear that there is no parity even amongst the 'African' languages of the 11 official ones, because some are smaller regional resources and others are 'larger' in their spread and value (Tshivenda, for example, as compared to isiZulu). And, 'within' these resources called official ('African') languages, there are some ways of use that are considered authentic and some that are considered corruptions, despite the inherent fluidity and dynamism of all social resources and practices, language included. Such categories of good and bad, it turns out, are really ones of social value, not of linguistic merit, per se.

Patrick (2007) and Mufwene (2006) have spelt out some of the problems with 'language endangerment' and 'language rights' discourses, summarised as follows: Such discourses tend to romanticise and reify language and cultures; language issues get cut off from the historical, political and economic context in which speakers find themselves; the mobility and social complexity of speakers gets sidelined; and such unifying and homogenising processes risk excluding and marginalising minorities or mobile people whose identity is not defined through older categories of ethnicity or speech community. If we drop the notion that languages are separate, living, boundaried beings, species or objects, they suggest, we make the study of language speakers and bilingualism a more complex but richer one, where they are situated by local and global forces, in particular socio-cultural, historical and economic environments. Patrick points out that linking language to a people and a tradition is often not in the interests of all speakers (2007: 124). Mufwene (2006: 137) asks whether there are 'language rights' independent of human rights. He points out that, as practice, languages are constantly being reshaped by their speakers and are not static. Where 'language shift' takes place, people have exercised the right to use the language resources of their choice. Why would people give up a resource that serves their communicative needs the best, he asks (Mufwene, 2006: 131). The rights of individuals and groups to pursue their interests under specific social conditions prevail over those of languages 'in themselves'. Governments cannot, in the end, control the day-to-day language practices of their populations. Education, however, is a 'border' or in-between zone, as far as language use goes, because it absorbs official policies around languages but is also subject to civil society influences regarding the different statuses of available linguistic resources. For example, that imagined bundle of linguistic resources that is commonly referred to as 'Standard English' usually has higher status than others in schooling and other formal settings but often not in other, less formal settings (Gee, 2007).

Language in Education Policy

Chapter 2 of the South African Constitution is a Bill of Rights, and in that chapter it stipulates that '(e)veryone has the right to receive education in the official language or languages of their choice in public educational institutions where that education is reasonably practicable' (Section 29). The operationalisation of these values first took place through the 1997 policy statement (Department of Education, 1997: 2) produced by the Ministry of Education that set out the direction for post-apartheid educational policy and curriculum development. There, the 'main aims' for language policy are described as being:

> to promote full participation in society and the economy through equitable and meaningful access to education; to pursue the language policy most supportive of general conceptual growth amongst learners, and hence to establish additive multilingualism as an approach to language in education; to promote and develop all the official languages; to support the teaching and learning of all other languages required by learners or used by communities in South Africa, including languages used for religious purposes, languages which are important for international trade and communication, and South African Sign Language, as well as Alternative and Augmentative Communication; to counter disadvantages resulting from different kinds of mismatches between home languages and languages of learning and teaching; and to develop programmes for the redress of previously disadvantaged languages.

The last five words of the quote pinpoint the 'language rights' claim, as well as its fragility – the idea of a language as a 'previously disadvantaged' persona is a very odd claim indeed, in the light of my earlier point that it is people, not languages, who compete and cooperate with each other, claim rights and experience advantage or disadvantage. The policy statement briefly reviews arguments for 'single medium', 'home language' education and 'dual medium' (or 'two-way immersion') programmes, and then says:

> Whichever route is followed, the underlying principle is to maintain home language(s) while providing access to and the effective acquisition

of additional language(s). Hence, the Department's position that an additive approach to bilingualism is to be seen as the normal orientation of our language-in-education policy.

The policy statement confirms the constitutional right of individuals to choose the language of learning, but cautions that this right has to 'be exercised within the overall framework of the obligation on the education system to promote multilingualism' (Department of Education, 1997: Preamble, p. 1, clause 2.6).

The Working Group on Values in Education that contributed closely to the formulation of the policy on language in the 1997 document, in their report to the Minister of Education entitled 'Values, Education and Democracy', identified

two main values we wish to promote in the area of language, which are, firstly, the importance of studying through the language one knows best, or as it is popularly referred to, mother-tongue education, and secondly, the fostering of multilingualism. We do believe that an initial grounding in mother-tongue learning is a pedagogically sound approach to learning. We also believe that multicultural communication requires clear governmental support and direction. (Section 4: Multilingualism)

The 1997 statement presents its language in education policy as being 'an integral and necessary aspect of the new government's strategy of building a non-racial nation in South Africa'. It is intended to facilitate 'communication across the barriers of colour, language and region, while at the same time creating an environment in which respect for languages other than one's own would be encouraged' (Department of Education, 1997: Preamble, p. 1, clause 3). 'Mother tongue' education as a 'values'-based strategy is thus presented as a reactive strategy to the segregated and discriminatory history of South Africa leading in to the 1990s. The statement assumes that people speak a language at home (say, isiXhosa or Afrikaans) which is the same as the standardised version of that language that counts at school, but this is even less the case for smaller African languages than it is for English, because they are less visible than English in formal and bureaucratic contexts and their standard versions are thus hardly visible at all outside of school settings.

These statements of policy and principle rely on a set of linked constructs such as 'home language', 'mother tongue', 'additional language', 'an additive approach to bilingualism' and 'additive multilingualism'. To these are added the terms that become ubiquitous in later policy statements and discussions, namely 'language of learning and teaching' (LOLT), 'dual' and 'single' language mediums of education. They all draw on what Heller (2007) has called a 'common-sense' but in fact highly ideologised view of bilingualism, where the conception is that of the co-existence of two (or more) linguistic systems. Heller and others (Lin, 1997; Martin-Jones, 2007; Michael-Luna & Canagarajah, 2007) bring into question the monodiscursive-monolingual norms implicit in such concepts. In a review of debates about bilingual education Martin-Jones (2007: 167) points out that a good deal of the policy-driven research has shown a strong preference for the construction of parallel monolingual spaces for learning, with strict monitoring of those spaces for their monolingualism. A major research direction in bilingual education has been around what kinds of programmes using language separation approaches or concurrent language approaches produced what kinds of successes for student learning and achievement. She points to what she calls a 'container metaphor of competence' manifest in terms like 'full bilingual competence', 'balanced bilingualism', 'additive bilingualism' and 'subtractive bilingualism', in effect all conceiving of languages and linguistic competencies as separate containers, side by side, that are more or less full or empty.

These influences surface strongly in the commitment to an 'additive bilingual' approach in the 1997 education policy statement for South Africa. That, in turn, drew from the National Education Policy Investigation (NEPI) group working on language. The NEPI researcher who summarised the proposal for an additive bilingual education model for South Africa, drawing on the Canadian work of Cummins (e.g. 1981), defined additive bilingualism as 'a form of bilingualism in which the person's first language is maintained while adding competence in another language' (Luckett, 1992: 4–5, quoted in Heugh, 1995: 334). She went on to advocate a 'transitional bilingualism model' 'in which, though the aim is to produce competence in a foreign language, the indigenous languages are used for initial education and are to some extent maintained'. As Heugh (1995: 334) pointed out, this model, despite Luckett's intentions, is very close to the 'subtractive model' where 'home language' is dropped altogether after a while in favour of the dominant language, and this is the interpretation given to her recommendations in the final NEPI report and implemented most commonly in educational practice since then. It is ironic, then, that policies which start from the position of celebrating diversity produce policies that institutionalise separation. These policies are helpless in the face of widespread social consensus that 'English' is a dominant set of linguistic resources in South African society, as it is in many other parts of the world, in 'English-speaking' societies, as well as many 'non-English speaking' societies, as other authors in this volume testify.

English Language Dominance and 'the English They Can Get'

English is indeed the elephant in the room, only obliquely referred to in these policy stipulations. It is English that is predominantly the preferred language of learning across schools and universities in South Africa, notwithstanding small but innovative African-language educational initiatives developed in Limpopo province, the Western Cape and elsewhere. The stipulation in the policy documents for 'learner choice' (or parental choice) in identifying their chosen LOLT allows for English to be selected ubiquitously as the LOLT and for regional education departments to proceed with the wide use of English language resources (with Afrikaans-medium instruction fighting for survival in tertiary education and with small pockets of experimentation providing instruction in other regional languages at school level). There is a second problem regarding the relationship between, on the one hand, so-called 'home languages' or 'mother tongue' as the language that is actually spoken in homes and local neighbourhoods, and, on the other hand, what counts as 'mother tongue' in schools and classrooms. Research undertaken in primary schools in the Western Cape shows students and teachers communicating by way of language forms that diverge from the standard isiXhosa in which the students will be tested (Xhalisa, 2011). My focus here, though, for the remaining discussion, is on the question of the dominance of English as the language of choice in schooling and higher education. Having argued that there are mistaken assumptions in policy outputs about languages and their use, when seen from a social practices perspective, I turn to an examination of classroom language. My focus is on an 'English' which is a form of bounded monolingual practice, endorsed and sustained in schools. My aim is not to show English as dominant but to examine how what counts as English is in fact both diverse and specific. The data reported on here is taken from a series of linked qualitative, ethnographic-style studies on post-foundation phase classroom literacy and language practices. The data comprises recorded instances of classroom interaction and detailed fieldnotes, and the methodological orientation has been that of interpretative linguistic and literacy ethnography (Heath & Street, 2008).

The following presents a typical scenario from a school where the teacher and students struggle to work with resources that are barely available to them. The teacher had copied a maths exercise from a book onto the blackboard and was now trying to help students with the problems they were having with the task. Neither the teacher nor the students had specialised English language resources that were appropriate for the task but nonetheless persevered by way of a particular, localised, monolingual English.

The background information for the exercise, taken from the textbook and copied onto the blackboard, reads as follows:

A farmer wishes to build a rectangular enclosure PQRS to house his chickens. He wants the area to be 200 square metres. One of the sides, namely, PS is along the wall of an existing building. The remaining three sides must be fenced. Fencing material costs R100 per square metre. He wants to calculate the dimensions of the rectangle so that he spends as little money as possible on fencing.

This is clearly not simply a maths problem for students with limited resources in the designated language, but also a problem of grasping what the practices are that are being signalled here and what the rules of engagement are. The teacher's explanation is given in Figure 2.1.

The teacher struggled to find the words in monolingual English to explain the point clearly to his Grade 10 maths class. For example, he did not make it clear to them what the phrase 'existing wall' indicated, even though

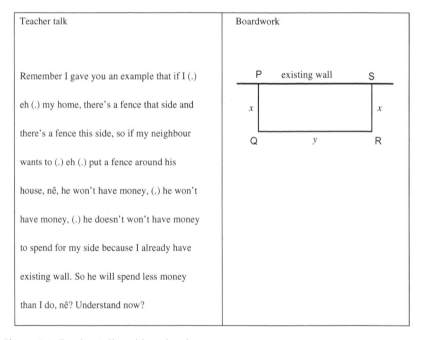

Teacher talk	Boardwork
Remember I gave you an example that if I (.)	
eh (.) my home, there's a fence that side and	
there's a fence this side, so if my neighbour	
wants to (.) eh (.) put a fence around his	
house, nê, he won't have money, (.) he won't	
have money, (.) he doesn't won't have money	
to spend for my side because I already have	
existing wall. So he will spend less money	
than I do, nê? Understand now?	

Figure 2.1 Teacher talk and boardwork
Note: (.) indicates a pause or a hesitancy

this was not an everyday term that the students might have picked up elsewhere. He struggled to find the language resources to explain that the farmer would not need to spend money on fencing the side where there was already a wall ('he won't have money, he won't have money, he doesn't won't have money to spend for my side' – his attempts here to find an appropriate verb phrase to explain the point falter and fail, ending with the incoherent and ungrammatical 'doesn't won't' conclusion).

Despite their struggles to absorb and understand, the students observed the rules of engagement and responded by attempting English themselves. Similarly, in their discussion of a case study of language in a similar township high school in the same locality, Blommaert et al. (2005: 392) reported that almost without exception 'the students expressed a great desire to learn English'. In support, they cite one piece of student writing as follows:

the language that I like at school to learn English because that Everybody they learn English because is a very nice language to Everyone that they want to speak English.

Blommaert (2007: 14) claims that

the situation is tragically clear: the township pupils – overwhelmingly black or 'colored' and poor – pin their hopes for upward social mobility on English; but *this particular English* (the one they *have* and the one they *can get*) is not going to allow them to achieve that goal. It is indeed the English they can get: their teachers also had no mastery of the elite varieties of English.

Blommaert's argument is that English exists in such post-colonial contexts on 'different scales'. The elite and their children have access to prestige varieties of spoken and written language while the mass of students have access only to 'sub-standard varieties that are only valid locally'. He concludes that 'the "world" language, in other words, exists in at least two – scaled – forms: one, a genuinely "globalised" English that connects elites worldwide, and another, a very local variety that offers very little translocal mobility' (Blommaert, 2007: 14–15).

English and Social Mobility

I would suggest, however, that while Blommaert accurately identifies the extent of the desire for English language education in certain urban settings (but not shared amongst all youths in less urban settings), the 'local' is itself layered into more complex scales of access and influence than is suggested by a simple juxtaposition between two scales. Fataar's (2009) research identifies the high levels of mobility that characterise students' movements across the city of Cape Town and surroundings, as they go in search of affordable and quality education. He examines the complex ways that township students access both suburban and township schools from beyond the confines of their immediate neighbourhoods. He suggests that the community school, 'the one nearby' has come to be seen as inferior and to be shunned in favour of schools *elsewhere*, suggesting a gap between official planning and the 'popular energies' which evade them. He describes a complex dispersal of students every morning on diverse paths from township to suburban schools and across township schools, in search of better schools. He talks of 'an affective disconnection between their places of living and their spaces of schooling' (Fataar, 2009: 3). His discussion points us to the observation that, as far as language goes, 'the one nearby' is similarly seen as inferior, as urban students and parents see quality education as happening in the prestige language varieties which they do not 'have'.

'English' In-between

In-between the scales of English language middle-class schools and failing township schools are a range of differently positioned schools, responding to the new demands and mobility that characterise the schooling terrain in the city. The excerpt below is from one of these repositioned ex-elite, suburban schools and shows a different kind of English-medium instruction to the struggling township school referenced above, but also very different from the middle-class schools near it. Like many other similar schools, this suburban school was formerly an all-white, middle-class 'Model C' school. It has become a relatively low fee-paying school that attracts working class black and coloured students who are dropped off/bused in by their parents from the townships and from the Cape Flats. There is also a small number of immigrant/refugee students from the Congo, Zimbabwe and elsewhere in Africa. The language of learning and teaching is monolingual English, but it is not the relaxed, at-home kind of English spoken in the more expensive middle-class schools near it. Most of the teaching happens at this school on the assumption that the children bring almost nothing with them to the school by way of linguistic resources and background knowledge. The lesson extract presented here is from a Grade 6 class. The teacher focuses on surface features of language and literacy coding and decoding and on surface features of language meanings. She carefully takes students through a reading aloud exercise and then makes them look up the meanings of words. There is no sense here that there is anything from the students' own worlds that might have relevance and the sole focus is on surface levels of comprehension.

(...) indicates a phrase that is inaudible on the recording

1	TEACHER:	Right. Ehm, we going to read this story. What can be so interesting about it? OK, I'm gonna, eh – Sipho starts, eh, then Marita, then Mishali, then Lorato. OK? Just three lines. Ok I'll tell you when to stop.
2	STUDENT:	[Starts reading] A turtle is a member of the reptile family. It is covered by scales and flakes. It is cold-blooded and breathes air. The outstanding feature of the turtle is its hard shell. This shell can be up to a metre long and is made from ribbed bones, covered with flakes or scales.
3	TEACHER:	Thank you. Who was the next one that I (...) Marita.
4	STUDENT:	[Reads] A turtle cannot pull its head into the shell like the tortoise, which is a close relative. There are seven types of marine turtle in the world, but most live in the warm tropical islands.
5	TEACHER:	OK. Thank you. No – finish that sentence.
6	STUDENT:	where they feed on algae and sea grasses.
7	TEACHER:	OK. Right. Go on.
8	STUDENT:	Turtles will spend nearly all their time in the water, but the female will crawl onto a beach to lay the rubbery shell eggs in a hole in the sand and lays the eggs and covers -
9	TEACHER:	Shuh! You know what is wrong here? You know what is wrong here? Same thing that happened when we read that first that was so badly done. OK? The sentence is written and on the other side in the middle is a picture, and the sentence goes on, on the other side. OK? So, we will start there again.
10	STUDENT:	Turtles will spend nearly all their time in the shell – shell – (Recording: R school, Grade 6, 11 August 2009)

Students took turns reading aloud in this class and the teacher did all the 'filling in' – clarifying the content matter and providing background information. There was almost no evidence of any engagement with the material on the part of the students, and the teacher clearly saw her role as gently inducing children to gain familiarity with the language resources which they did not have. The teacher's intervention in Turn 9 is about a reading error where the student misread because the sentence jumped across a picture on the page. The student was apparently simply reading the words rather than the sense of the writing and so did not notice that 'and lays the eggs and covers' (Turn 8) does not follow grammatically from the earlier sentence fragment. The attention to reading as print-based produced a focus which rendered the image of the turtle laying her eggs as redundant and also produced a misreading. This is closer to what Williams (1996) called a 'reading-like' activity than to a reading activity because of the focus on surface features of language and text rather than on meaning. Language and literacy approximate here to the high status resources that are on display in the elite classrooms but they do not set an effective basis for the making and taking of meanings and understandings in other contexts, because they are cut off from the requisite that meanings are made in contexts of relevance and exchange, if they are to link up to or provide bridges for related activities in other contexts. They are, however, of a different order of social indexicality to the township classroom interactions – they provide limited access to the high status resources sought, whereas the township classroom examined provided almost no access at all. Thus, while the learning and teaching do not provide a direct version of the high status resources associated with the privileged versions of the elite schools, they promise at least access to greater mobility at the local and regional level.

In contrast, we can look at the following extract taken from a school in the suburbs where the students are predominantly middle class and mostly, but not exclusively, white. The school charges fees which are high but not at the same level as the handful of 'top' schools nearby which excel every year on the national league tables of school-leavers who attain distinctions in their examinations. So this is a comfortably middle-class school but not in the first league of such schools.

As can be seen in the data I examine below, there is no bridging of in-school and out-of-school language resources for these students because there is not assumed to be a gulf. In the sense that Heath (1983) made this argument, the school is an extension and elaboration of their home community's ways of knowing and being, and this is reflected in the language of the classroom. In the following extract the teacher has enriched the Silent Uninterrupted Reading Exercise (SURE), where students engage in quiet novel reading every day for 15 minutes, by bringing in a hot drink in response to the cold weather, on a day when an unusually high percentage of students are absent during a seasonal flu outbreak.

1	**TEACHER:**	... I've decided today is Hot Chocolate day while we have ... um ... SURE reading ... but the deal is that this is a privilege. I went to the shop and took my own money and bought this for you because I love you so much, so don't abuse them. (...) alright?
2	**STUDENT:**	(noise and all talking simultaneously) Thank you miss!
3	**TEACHER:**	(...) And thank you to Jean and Claire who helped in the background.
4	**TEACHER:**	O.K. guys, please don't burn yourselves and please don't mess.
5	**STUDENT:**	Is there sugar in?
6	**STUDENT:**	I'm not supposed to drink hot chocolate and sugar ...
7	**STUDENT:**	It makes you hyper (...)
8	**STUDENT:**	(Various talking simultaneously) Is this is an experiment miss?
9	**TEACHER:**	The experiment is to see how brave you children are when there's teachers present (...). (A reference to the researcher at the back of the classroom)
10	**STUDENT:**	(Various talking simultaneously)
11	**STUDENT:**	What is this?
12	**TEACHER:**	This is LO.
13	**STUDENT:**	LO?
14	**TEACHER:**	Developing the skill of being grateful
15	**STUDENT:**	How about we do an experiment to see how hyper I can (be) with 3 cups of coffee .... (Recording: P school, Grade 7, 5 August 2009)

The chatty and interactive nature of the exchanges suggests a common ease with the setting and form of communication. There is a sense that things are being negotiated and there is room for students to talk amongst themselves while the teacher maintains a loose authority through the exchanges. In Line 1 the teacher adopts a nurturing, intimate familial tone (... 'because I love you so much') together with the teacherly warning about 'not getting out of hand'. Notably, only one student actually carried out the task of reading a novel during the whole period, whereas the others chatted amongst themselves without upsetting their teacher. So the 'literacy work' was not an issue for the teacher. She seemed more concerned that the students relaxed and interacted within the boundaries that she set. The student question in line 8 ('Is this an experiment miss?') started a joking dialogue where teacher and students played with words in a relaxed way: The teacher's answer about it being an experiment 'to see how brave you are' (line 9) was both a reminder to the students that they and the teacher were under observation from the researcher but also an invitation to them to be assertive and entertaining. In response to a similar question (line 11, What is this?) the teacher makes an 'insider' joke about it being LO. Life Orientation (LO) is a school subject on the new curriculum, intended to be about developing 'life skills'. (Teachers are sometimes uncertain about LO as a school subject, finding it too 'unacademic' or too 'personal' in its focus or not convinced as to its place on the timetable – at this school boys and girls are often separated into separate LO classes to discuss sex education, HIV/AIDS, 'body-care' and related topics.) The last exchange (line 15) is an example of an intertextual moment where the student playfully ventriloquates (or double-voices, in the Bhaktininian sense) parental/medicalised conversations about youthful activity as sugar-induced hyperactivity. This last joke closes the circle started by the teacher expressing her (*in loco parentis*) love for her students as the student now invokes the parental 'voice' directly and maintains a teenagerly 'attitude' of her own.

For students at the school from social backgrounds that are not white or middle class the language of the school is gently assimilationist. Fataar (2009: 7) described teachers at a similar school in Cape Town as seeing it as 'their morally ordained duty to educate for middleclass civility'. In their own words, he says, they are 'race blind', or they 'don't see race'. Fataar suggests that 'this stance prevents constructive mediation of racial and cultural difference from becoming part of the school's reference world, which precludes the productive incorporation of difference into the school's functional culture'. He suggests that 'assimilation into the pre-existing culturally white ethos of the school is as much facilitated by the white teachers at the school as by the non-engagement of parents who are spatially (they live elsewhere in the city) and conceptually distant'.

The language of the school is, of course, English, and the teacher moves fluidly in and out of more formal genres and registers and 'everyday English'. The excerpt below shows a teacher at Grade 6 level familiarising children with 'rap' as a poetry/performance genre which, however, has been cleaned up, is monolingual and shorn of any youth-cultural/oppositional/'gangsta credentials'.

T: Rhyming. Okay. So it says: 'Everybody rap.' If you look at the pictures here of the two guys, right, that would obviously have been 'cool' about twenty years ago, when they rapped, right? {pupils laugh.} Rappers today don't look like that. They wear these funny sunglasses. Their hair's all funny and that but that's only their stage personality, right¿ If you see them in the street or when you see them going out with their friends, they are dressed normally. Right¿ But for this particular, ehm, for their stage persona they have, (.) a certain rapping style. The way they dress. The way they walk. Rappers don't walk onto the stage, wait, they have a ... {The Teacher demonstrates the way the rappers walk. The whole class laughs. The Teacher has to raise the level of her voice.} ... you know what I'm saying¿ Okay, Karl , /../ ja. 'Everybody rap. Can you do a rap¿ Can you do a rap¿ Can you make a rhyme¿ Can you make a rhyme¿' {The Teacher addresses the class.} What are we doing there¿

PP: They're repeating themselves.

T: Repeating. A rap song is all about¿ (.) repeating. Why do you remember rap songs, or even pop songs¿ Because they sing the same thing over and over again. The chorus they sing a few times. The (.) they use the same, eh, words in different, eh, verses. Right¿ So it's easy to remember. Also the tune, it's very catchy. It's got a funky beat. Right. I'll go through the next few lines.
Can you link up words¿
Can you link up words¿
To help me blow my mind.
To help me blow my mind.
Poetry is a thing we can do
to show that there is no difference.
Between me and you.
Black and White are all the same
and those who say different are mad insane.
Do you agree¿ Do you agree¿
If you agree, say Ja to me.
So I want you. (.) to think of ways that you in your pairs can rap this out. (..) Okay¿ You going to, eh, work through it now. Brainstorm ideas. Ehm, you can write on the page. You can say who's going to say which lines, etc. and then, ehm, you can have it ready for me for next week. That's, (.) this will be your final assessment mark for this term (.) (Recording: P school, Grade 7, 30 July 2009)

On one level the teacher's language is fluid and dialogical. She loots stereotypes from popular culture to draw the children in to engaging with her theme. She uses her body and models what she wants the children to do. But rap music gets stripped of any alternative, oppositional potential and becomes just one kind of simple poetry display, and the topic for an examinable piece of writing. The teacher locates rap in a context-free limbo from 20 years previously. It is worth noting here that there is a vibrant rap/hip hop, primarily township musical tradition in South Africa, known as *kwaito*, that meshes African language resources with English, Afrikaans and *escamto* or *tsotsitaal*, but it is precisely their mobile mix that disqualifies them from classroom use.

My argument in this discussion of data from three different classrooms has been that 'English' is something different in different school settings, depending on the situated resources and intentions of social actors. On the basis of these examples we can concur with Martin-Jones (2007: 174) that children (and teachers) who already have knowledge of prestige varieties of English from out of school are positioned advantageously in comparison to poorer students who do not have that access. From this perspective, the language practices of schooling can be said to reproduce existing relations of dominance as the interactional routines of classrooms link to the wider social and ideological order. But English does not operate simply as either a 'standard' variety, which the children of the elite have access to and practice in school, or a 'sub-elite' version, which the children of the poor have to assimilate. Both the social conditions and the language resources used are more variable and complex than that two-tiered model would allow.

Conclusion

From language policy documents we read the intentions and hopes of the policy writers that language will serve as an instrument that will help to bring about more equal access to greater resources and a 'levelling of the playing fields'. From the classroom exchanges examined here we see the vulnerable underbelly of these policies. As Mufwene (2006) pointed out, governments cannot control the day-to-day language practices of their populations. Nor do languages go extinct the way plant or animal species die out. Instead, they change and shift in relation to the social context – the economic, cultural and political milieu in which language users find themselves. Rather than existing as policy instruments that can be employed to bring about social objectives, languages are barometers, in their relative statuses, scales of uses and productivity, of the character and ranges of inequalities and contests that characterise the wider social setting. Effective policy-making should be based on a closer understanding of how language is practiced, rather than relying on projections onto particular 'languages' of romanticized and essentialised notions of language-culture and indigeneity.

Notes

(1) A grant by the National Research Foundation in South Africa supported the field-work part of this study. I acknowledge here the contributions of Nicola Pietersen and Thabisa Xhalisa as grant-supported student researchers on the project. This chapter is an extension and revision of an earlier paper entitled 'The Odd Couple: Diverging Paths in Language Policy and Educational Practices' that was published in *Perspectives in Education*, 2011, 29 (4) 1–9.

(2) They are, of course, Sepedi, Sesotho, Setswana, siSwati, Tshivenda, Xitsonga, Afrikaans, English, isiNdebele, isiXhoza and isiZulu. The 2001 population census was the last national report on language distribution. Based on a question which asked respondents to name the language they spoke predominantly at home, the breakdown was as follows: In a then population of 44.8 million in South Africa, 23.8% spoke IsiZulu; 17.6% spoke IsiXhosa; 13.3% spoke Afrikaans; 9.4% spoke Sepedi; 8.2% spoke Setswana; 8.2% spoke English; 7.9% spoke Sesotho; 4.4% spoke Xitsonga; 2.7% spoke SiSwati; 2.3% spoke Tshivenda; 1.6% spoke IsiNdebele. The census data has since been criticised for the essentialist construction of language it utilised, which assumed that people were monolingual speakers at home. Evidence of language shift and the widening of existing linguistic repertoires have been described since then, showing a more complicated breakdown and distribution of linguistic resources in multilingual settings (Deumert, 2010).

References

Austin, J.L. (1975) *How To Do Things With Words.* Cambridge, MA: Harvard University Press.

Blommaert, J. (2005) Situating language rights: English and Swahili in Tanzania revisited. *Journal of Socio-linguistics* 9 (3), 390–417.

Blommaert, J. (2007) Socio-linguistic scales. *Intercultural Pragmatics* 4 (1), 1–19.

Blommaert, J., Muyllaert, N., Huysmans, M. and Dyers, C. (2005) Peripheral normativity: Literacy and the production of locality in a South African township school. *Linguistics and Education* 16 (4), 378–403.

Bourdieu, P. (1991) *Language and Symbolic Power.* Cambridge, MA: Harvard University Press.

Constitution of South Africa, SA Govt Act 108 (1996), accessed 2 January 2010. Online at http://www.info.gov.za/documents/constitution/1996/a108-96.pdf.

Cummins, J. (1981) Empirical and theoretical underpinnings of bilingual education. *Journal of Education* 163, 16–127.

Department of Education (1997) *Language in Education Policy*, accessed 3 January 2010. Online at http://us-cdn.creamermedia.co.za/assets/articles/attachments/04391_language_in_education.pdf; http://cyberserv.co.za/users/~jako/lang/education.htm.

Deumert, A. (2010) Tracking the demographics of (urban) language shift an analysis of South African census data. *Journal of Multilingual and Multicultural Development* 31 (1), 13–35.

Duranti, A. (2010) Linguistic anthropology: Language as a non-neutral medium. In R. Mesthrie (ed.) *The Cambridge Handbook of Socio-linguistics.* Cambridge: Cambridge University Press, accessed 3 January 2010. Online at http://www.sscnet.ucla.edu/anthro/faculty/duranti/Non-neutral%20medium.pdf.

Fataar, A. (2009) Schooling subjectivities across the post-apartheid city. *Africa Education Review* 6 (1), 1–18.

Gee, J.P. (2007) *Social Linguistics and Literacies: Ideology in Discourses* (3rd edn). New York: Taylor and Francis.

Gumperz, J. and Hymes, D. (1972) *Directions in Socio-linguistics: The Ethnography of Communication*. New York: Holt, Rinehart and Winston.

Heath, S. (1983) *Ways with Words: Language, Life and Work in Communities and Classrooms*. Cambridge: Cambridge University Press.

Heath, S. and Street, B. (2008) *On Ethnography: Approaches to Language and Literacy Research*. New York: Teachers College Press.

Heller, M. (2007) *Bilingualism: A Social Approach*. Basingstoke: Palgrave Macmillan.

Heugh, K. (1995) Disabling and enabling: Implications of language policy trends in South Africa. In R. Mesthrie (ed.) *Language and Social History* (pp. 329–350). Cape Town: David Philip.

Lin, A. (1997) Hong Kong children's rights to a culturally compatible English education. *Hong Kong Journal of Applied Linguistics* 2 (2), 23–48, accessed 3 January 2010. Online at http://sunzi.lib.hku.hk/hkjo/view/5/500026.pdf.

Luckett, K. (1992) Additive bilingualism: New models of language education for South African schools. Working paper. Cape Town: Language Policy Research Group of the National Education Policy Investigation.

Makoni, S. and Pennycook, A. (2007) *Disinventing and Reconstituting Languages*. Clevedon: Multilingual Matters.

Martin-Jones, M. (2007) Bilingualism, education and the regulation of access to language resources. In M. Heller (ed.) *Bilingualism: A Social Approach* (pp. 161–182). Basingstoke: Palgrave Macmillan.

Michael-Luna, S. and Canagarajah, S. (2007) Multilingual academic literacies: Pedagogical foundations for code meshing in primary and higher education. *Journal of Applied Linguistics* 4 (1), 55–77.

Ministry of Education (2002) *Language Policy for Higher Education*, accessed 3 January 2010. Online at http://www.education.gov.za/content/documents/67.pdf.

Mufwene, S. (2006) Language endangerment: An embarrassment for linguistics. *Proceedings from the Annual Meeting of the Chicago Linguistic Society* 42 (2), 111–140, accessed 3 January 2010. Online at http://cls.metapress.com/content/j706830l02558n5k/.

Patrick, D. (2007) Language endangerment, language rights and indigeneity. In M. Heller (ed.) *Bilingualism: A Social Approach* (pp. 111–134). Basingstoke: Palgrave Macmillan.

Street, B. (1984) *Literacy in Theory and Practice*. Cambridge: Cambridge University Press.

Values, Education and Democracy (2000) Report of the Working Group on Values in Education. Online at http://www.info.gov.za/otherdocs/2000/education.htm. Accessed 3 January 2010.

Williams, E. (1996) Reading in two languages at year five in African primary schools. *Applied Linguistics* 17 (2), 182–209.

Xhalisa, T. (2011) Educators' perceptions of and practices around early instruction and language issues in a Cape Town township primary school. Masters Minor Dissertation, University of Cape Town.

3 The Rise and Rise of English: The Politics of Bilingual Education in Australia's Remote Indigenous Schools

Ilana Snyder and Denise Beale

Introduction

In September 2009, the ABC's (Australian Broadcasting Corporation) flagship current affairs TV show *Four Corners* examined the Northern Territory government's decision to dismantle bilingual education programmes in remote indigenous communities. Debbie Whitmont (2009) began her report with the observation that when it comes to selling Australia as a tourist destination in Qantas advertisements, Aboriginal language is part of Australian identity, but in the classrooms of the Northern Territory, indigenous languages are not in favour, again; state policy has fluctuated over time. When the 2008 national literacy tests found that four out of five children in remote schools did not meet basic standards of English literacy (NTDET, 2009), the Northern Territory government blamed bilingual schooling and the Minister for Education determined that from January 2009 all schools had to teach the first four hours each day in English (Scrymgour, 2008).

Bilingual Education and English Language in Context

Despite some criticism in the media, the government did not back down. The Chief Minister for the Northern Territory told Whitmont that he supported the policy: 'We are not banning the speaking of Indigenous languages, the teaching of Indigenous culture in our schools. What we are saying explicitly is that we should have the same expectations for these kids to get to benchmark in years 3, 5, 7 and 9 along with all other kids' (Whitmont, 2009).

Four Corners examined the rationale behind bilingual education. The first formal bilingual programmes in the Northern Territory aimed at preserving the few remaining indigenous languages. In the words of a teacher who had run a bilingual programme in the 1970s: 'You only learn to read once. Once a child can learn to read his own language and can write it properly and can speak English, then we'll try to teach the child to read English as well.' Another teacher who had taught in a bilingual programme in the 1980s emphasised: 'It's not just a bilingual school but a bicultural school .... Sometimes old women come along and tell sand stories sitting outside and demonstrate making of wooden artefacts. Without them we couldn't have the culture side of the program whatsoever' (Whitmont, 2009).

Four Corners also examined how bilingual education had performed in two Aboriginal communities, Lajamanu and Yirrkala. When Whitmont asked locals in Lajamanu how the new policy of making English the dominant teaching language would impact on the students, those interviewed felt that their view had been ignored and their culture devalued: 'It's like when you lose your loved ones, you feel the same way when you lose your language,' said Zachariah Patterson, a local community spokesperson. 'Well I think language is a large part of people's identity and their pride in who they are,' said Wendy Baarda, another local community member (Whitmont, 2009).

By contrast, Whitmont's visit to Yirrkala produced a very different picture. Yirrkala is a community in north-east Arnhem Land with a long cultural tradition and a strong view about preserving its language. The community has produced some of Australia's best known Aboriginal leaders, including the musician Mandawuy Yunupingu who oversaw bilingual education as a former principal at the school. At Yirrkala, leaders of the community told *Four Corners* they would not be taking any notice of the minister's directive. In the words of a community leader, Djuwalpi Marika: 'They want to westernise Yolngu people, they want to leave us in the mainstream culture like a whiteman. We don't want to live like that' (Whitmont, 2009).

The current affairs programme reflected the considerable media interest in the issue: there was extensive coverage in the *Australian*, the national Murdoch broadsheet, and in the Fairfax papers, as well as on radio, television and the internet, including programmes targeted at indigenous communities (Calma, 2009). The Minister for Education's decision aroused strong responses from proponents of bilingual education as documented on *Four Corners*. But, there was also opposition, as exemplified by the header 'Separatist schooling failure in the NT' (Hughes & Hughes, 2008), in the *Australian*.

Over the following months the Northern Territory's decision was supported by the federal government, most notably in comments by the Deputy Prime Minister and Minister for Education, Julia Gillard (*The Age*, 2008), and opposed by many others, including indigenous educators and community leaders, the Human Rights Commissioner, Tom Calma, and linguists and organisations associated with education (Devlin, 2009; Simpson *et al.*, 2009).

In this chapter we explore the radical change in policy from a number of perspectives. We begin with some of the value-laden understandings of language and literacy education that informed the decision to mandate the four hours policy. We then turn to the relationship between English and indigenous languages from a historical perspective. Next, the discussion moves to bilingualism and its educational appeal. This is followed by a brief consideration of the often contested policy initiatives that have established programmes in remote communities. The final section focuses on the complex political forces that contributed to the official demise of bilingual programmes in 2008, ending on a note of qualified optimism for the future.

Views of Language that Prevailed

Despite its multicultural nature Australia has only one official language, English, although several hundred languages are spoken within Australian homes. In the Northern Territory, in 2006, 26% of its residents, approximately 50,000 people, spoke a language other than English as their first language, with 15% of these being indigenous (ABS, 2008).

The shift in policy from using both indigenous languages and English to only English in the first four hours of the school day and then indigenous languages in the remaining sessions affected fewer than 20% of schools in the sparsely populated Northern Territory. That the shift elicited so much attention illustrates the deeply political and value-laden nature of language and language policy: questions of power, ideology and politics are central (Bell & Stevenson, 2006). To mandate that English should become the language of instruction in all Northern Territory schools was to ascribe the low achievement in English, literacy in English and numeracy amongst indigenous students, as measured on standardised tests, to the use of their own language, that is, to view language as separate from the historical, social and cultural conditions that have influenced and shaped it.

There was also no recognition in the decision of the complex issues associated with high-stakes literacy testing: that literacy tests and the apparatus of testing are never neutral (Street, 1984, 1997). Despite the best efforts of test makers, some children possess the cultural and social capital that helps them to understand the particular language associated with testing and to decode the questions, but for others, such as students in remote communities for whom English is often their second, third or fourth language (Wilkins, 2008), there are no such advantages. Although there is much research evidence to suggest that differences in literacy achievement as measured by standardised tests need to be approached with caution, this was not the case in the Northern Territory in 2008 (Snyder, 2008). Making the use of English compulsory was the Minister's solution because through it she believed that literacy would be imparted. A political act that embodied a superficially populist appeal, it resolutely ignored the many factors that undermine English literacy achievement, including, at the very least, location, health, school attendance and languages spoken (Snyder, 2008).

Nor was there any understanding in the decision that to mandate English as the medium of instruction in remote indigenous schools invokes the conferred status of English in Australia and the relegation of indigenous languages and culture to an inferior position. The choice of English as the preferred medium also reflects the deep belief that from proficiency in English everything else follows. It is part of the longstanding mythology that surrounds literacy (Graff, 1993), which builds on the assumption that literacy in English is a set of basic skills that, once acquired, will change life prospects for individuals and groups in society – in the present case, for indigenous children in remote communities. Many potent effects are attributed to the acquisition of literacy in English – cognitive, social, behavioural and motivational. People who have a command of English are seen to be more creative, politically aware, aspiring. Proficiency in English is associated with moral character, discipline and order, and with economic growth, wealth and productivity. But even a superficial appraisal of Australian history confirms that literacy in English has not assured most indigenous Australians, whether located in urban, regional or remote areas, of any such advantages and social positioning.

The decision to mandate English as the medium of instruction was both a response and a reaction to federal government policy which portrayed the Northern Territory government as derelict in its duty to its indigenous inhabitants. But also manifest in the policy change was the deeply ambivalent attitude of the Australian state to indigenous languages and their intrinsic connection to indigenous culture and rights to self-determination.

English and Indigenous Languages

Before the arrival of the first Europeans in 1788, it is estimated that there were more than 300,000 indigenous people who spoke over 200 indigenous languages (HRSCATSUA, 1992). As the continent was colonised, many indigenous people died, their cultures were suppressed and English was imposed, with the resultant loss of the majority of the languages. Caffery (2002: 6) estimates that approximately 20 of those which remain are 'classed as strong languages, having between 500 and 3,000 speakers'. Also important to note is that the first language for many indigenous people is often Aboriginal English or Kriol (HRSCATSUA, 1992).

Official policy which deals with indigenous languages encounters the fundamental paradox of the Australian state – that it is built on the dispossession of the indigenous people (Wolfe, 1999). As a direct consequence, policy in this area is characterised by ambiguity. On the one hand, the importance of indigenous languages to indigenous identity is acknowledged, as is the significance of the loss of these languages (HRSCATSUA, 1992; Purdie *et al.*, 2008). On the other hand, indigenous languages are considered analogous to other languages used in multicultural Australian society, as expressed in the *National Statement [and Plan for Languages Education in Australian Schools 2005–08]* which 'affirms the value of *all* languages, including the importance of Australia's Indigenous languages' (Purdie *et al.*, 2008: 2).

The foundational policy text that informs contemporary decisions, the National Aboriginal and Torres Strait Islander Education Policy (AEP), implicitly recognises that indigenous languages are declining, but its commitment is no more than 'to develop programs to support the maintenance and continued use of Aboriginal and Torres Strait Islander Languages' (DEET, 1989: n.p.). Despite the existence of principles within numerous reports that could guide an articulated plan of support for indigenous languages, the reality is that their adoption as official policy would confront the Australian state with questions relating to the status of indigenous people as the first Australians and its role in their dispossession. This helps explain why official policies such as the AEP simply pose a statement of values.

Nowhere is this paradox more evident than in the Northern Territory where most of the indigenous language speakers live. In 2009, the Northern Territory's population was 224,800, in an Australian population of 22 million (ABS, 2009), of whom, in the 2006 census, approximately 26% spoke a first language other than English. Of those, 15.1% spoke an indigenous language as their first language, compared with 0.3% Australia-wide (ABS, 2008).

The Northern Territory Department of Education and Training notes that while 4.4% of school students on average across Australia are indigenous, the corresponding figure in the Northern Territory is 40.5%, of whom nearly half live in remote locations (NTDET, 2009). The larger number of indigenous students in the Northern Territory means that language is a salient issue for the educational authorities. In government schools the proportion of indigenous students is high with 47% indigenous, a figure that has grown by 4% in four years, reflecting a growing indigenous population (NTDET, 2009).

These aggregated figures highlight language as a vital issue but they obscure the diversity amongst indigenous people and communities within Australia. Ford (1996: 16) points out the multilingual and multicultural nature of indigenous populations, remarking that 'it is common for Aboriginal people to be multilingual and understand and use more than one Aboriginal language'. As well as differing languages, the cultures and histories of contact amongst indigenous groups are also varied (Wilkins, 2008), so while we use the term 'community' to refer to remote settlements and townships, we recognise the contested nature of the term. Further, its use implies a unity that may not exist (Commonwealth of Australia, 2008; Ford & Klesch, 2003; Kral & Falk, 2004) as these communities 'are, in fact, places where people have been forced to gather for many reasons which history and the marginalisation of Aboriginal Australia can testify to' (Ford & Klesch, 2003: 34).

The question of indigenous languages, their survival and continuing use is thus interwoven with the colonial past, marginalisation, identity and an assertion by indigenous people of their rights to maintain and revitalise their cultures and languages and, in so doing, gain greater control over their lives. The push for bilingual education programmes in remote schools in many ways has embodied this assertion of indigenous rights.

Reclaiming Language: Bilingual Education in Remote Communities

The impetus for formal bilingual education programmes in remote indigenous communities was connected to a global movement for the recognition of human rights following World War II and the processes of decolonisation (Attwood, 2005). The recognition of the rights and suffering of indigenous peoples was first given expression in UNESCO's Declaration of 1953 (Harris & Devlin, 1997). The developing human rights regime gave legitimacy and support to the struggles of indigenous people to gain control over their lands and the education of their children, and to protect and maintain their cultures and languages (Nakata, 2003).

In Australia, bilingual education programmes were part of moves to self-determination, which followed the fight for rights by Australian indigenous people – the fight for recognition, redress and land rights (Yunupingu, 1998). In remote Northern Territory indigenous communities, instruction in English was a legal requirement, despite the fact that most children spoke an indigenous language (Graham, 1999). For indigenous peoples, education in their own languages was a fundamental expression of their identity (Graham, 1999). For governments, bilingual education was seen as a means to raise indigenous peoples' standards of living, expressed in the US in 1968 in the Bilingual Education Act (Title VII of the Elementary and Secondary Education Act 1968, cited in Harris & Devlin, 1997). This Act strongly influenced the shape of the bilingual education programme conceived by the Whitlam government in 1972 (Harris & Devlin, 1997; HRSCATSUA, 1992).

While there are many definitions of bilingual education, May (2008: 20) argues that its defining feature is 'instruction *in* two languages'. The curriculum is delivered through both languages, distinguishing bilingual education from a language teaching programme in which the new language is the content to be taught (May, 2008). With the exception of French-immersion programmes in Canada that were initially designed for children from the anglophone majority, bilingual education typically denotes a specific population as it usually involves minority groups which may be constituted as potentially threatening within a particular nation state (Lo Bianco, 2008a). The minority language and the dominant one are both used for instruction, although the aim is often transitional – to shift to instruction in the national language. Bilingual education programmes such as these can be used with immigrant groups (e.g. Cahnmann & Varghese, 2005) or with minority ethnic groups (e.g. Jaffe, 2003).

The purpose of a bilingual programme is important. To add a new language is the primary goal, while building on the first language expands the students' cultural resources and is thus 'additive'. However, it can also be 'subtractive', aiming to shift students from a minority language to a dominant one as soon as practicable, thereby lessening the influence and strength of the mother tongue (Ernst-Slavit, 1997; May, 2008: 20). Another purpose is for 'maintenance', where instruction in the students' first language continues for a number of years, gradually incorporating the second language, with the goal of strengthening the first language and the cultural identity associated with it (May, 2008). This model is based partly on the ideas of Jim Cummins (1999), who believes that literacy is best acquired in the students' first language as it enables a more effective transfer of literacy to the second language (Collins, 1999; May, 2008).

Cummins (1999) points out that bilingual education in schools has always been controversial and highly politicised, particularly when the programmes involve minority or indigenous groups. These groups may achieve rights and privileges which can be perceived as not accruing to the majority of the population (c.f. May, 1998). In recent years, indigenous bilingual education programmes in remote communities have proven to be more contentious than the low numbers of students involved would suggest as they raise crucial questions around national sovereignty, particularly in an environment where land ownership and native title continue to be the focus of intense political, legislative and cultural contestation (e.g. Yunupingu, 1998).

As argued earlier, language is political. In Australia, English, as the language of the settlers, remains dominant and its acquisition enforced by the state, which ascribes to its use the properties of 'stability and social cohesion' (May, 1998: 273). This very dominance means that access to the resources that enable full participation in Australian society depend critically on a high degree of competence in English, both oral and written. Martin Nakata (2003: 14) points out the complexities of this position for indigenous and Torres Strait Islander people: they 'operate at the interface of two different cultures that have different histories and different worldviews'. The continuing experiences of colonisation and the conflicting demands of the state force cultural and linguistic change upon indigenous people, without necessarily endowing them with the requisite skills to enable them to succeed in the dominant culture.

In this context, the special worth of bilingual education programmes is to assert and maintain the value of the indigenous language through the legitimacy conferred on it by its use as a medium of instruction alongside the dominant language, English (May, 2008). The literacy practices that are created in the school, particularly the processes through which an oral language is transformed into a literate one, also legitimise the bodies of knowledge from which they are drawn, with culturally constitutive effects (Kral, 2009). In the Australian indigenous context, the work of Marika (2000) and of Ford and Klesch (2003) demonstrates the significance of these practices and processes. Kral (2009: 3) notes that 'in the Warlpiri region, the bilingual program gave Warlpiri families a strong sense of ownership and pride in their school and their children's learning'. The relationship between the minority and the dominant language, and the purposes for which each is used, may well follow different trajectories over time, with indigenous people using the new literacy practices in ways that are culturally meaningful for them (Jaffe, 2003; Murphy & Vencio, 2009). The experience of the bilingual programme can thus disrupt the historical legacy of alienation from schooling and society.

As mentioned above, the first official bilingual education programme began in the Northern Territory in 1973 at the instigation of the new federal Whitlam Labor government, which instituted a shift from the assimilationist policies that had dominated the preceding decades (Graham, 1999). The expression of a belief in the importance of indigenous language to culture and identity was given force in the development of bilingual education programmes in more than 20 schools between 1973 and 1983 (Harris & Devlin, 1997). The Northern Territory programmes in turn provided a model for other programmes throughout Australia (Harris & Devlin, 1997).

The aims of the bilingual education programmes were both the 'transfer and maintenance' of indigenous language and English literacy (Harris & Devlin, 1997: 4). A 'staircase' model was adopted, one in which literacy is developed first in the indigenous language, with English used orally, reflecting the influence of Cummins' ideas (Marika, 2000: 46). Each language was to be used for approximately 50% of the school day. Over time, the use of the indigenous language would gradually decrease and English literacy would be consolidated as the student moved through primary school (Harris & Devlin, 1997). Team-teaching with indigenous-speaking aides led to the development of both formal and informal programmes to train them as teachers (Harris & Devlin, 1997). As indigenous people became more involved as teachers, the purposes of the programme shifted to an increased focus on language and cultural maintenance (Harris & Devlin, 1997).

Yolŋu teacher-linguist Raymattja Marika depicts the establishment in 1975 of a bilingual education programme at Yirrkala Community Education Centre. Marika (2000: 47) illustrates the intense community involvement in the development of what she calls a '"both ways" curriculum .... The idea of "both ways" education means more than just having print literacy in two languages – it means having a strong emphasis on Yolŋu knowledge as well' (2000, 47). She describes 'a program of Aboriginalisation' (2000, 47), where the indigenous community took control of the curriculum as 'children have a right to know and understand their own cultural belief systems as well as the language and values of mainstream Balanda education' (2000, 51). Her conceptualisation incorporated English literacy, but with indigenous knowledge and language regarded as of equal importance.

The bilingual education programmes were not without their critics. A greater focus on literacy and numeracy at the federal and territory levels brought pressures for change in bilingual schools, giving force to Lo Bianco's (2008b: 351) assertion that 'policy changes in English literacy. ... impact on the teaching of indigenous languages, even if unintended'.

Testing Times: The Prioritisation of Literacy (in English)

In Australia, education policy, including indigenous education policy, is primarily the responsibility of the states and territories but, since the 1970s, the federal government has become increasingly influential. A specific focus on literacy and numeracy for indigenous learners emerged in federal policy in 1988 (Schwab, 1995) in the context of federal government concern over the general standard of education and a desire to reorient schools to serve more economic purposes (Dawkins, 1988). Improving standards of literacy and numeracy was seen as central to improving Australia's economic competitiveness. At the same time, an outcomes-based approach to schooling at the national level heralded moves to test school students' literacy and numeracy achievement.

In 1989, federal, state and territory governments agreed to national goals on schooling, integral to which was the improvement of literacy and numeracy performance for all school students (MCEECDYA, 2008: n.p.). By contrast, the National Aboriginal and Torres Strait Islander Education Policy of the same year focused on 'long term goals' to improve access to schooling for indigenous children (DEET, 1989).

The first National School English Literacy Survey undertaken in 1996 confirmed that indigenous students achieved the worst results in literacy tasks, although there was a wide divergence amongst states and territories (Commonwealth of Australia, 2000). Standards of literacy and numeracy were considered as key reasons for the poor educational outcomes of indigenous students, including lower school retention and the subsequent impact on future careers and options available to them (Commonwealth of Australia, 2000).

The need to improve literacy achievement amongst students in bilingual schools was the justification for the first move by the Northern Territory government to end bilingual education in 1998 at a time when 20 schools were delivering such programmes, even though there was little evidence of failure to achieve English literacy (Devlin, 1999). A strong public response against the decision led to a review of indigenous education in the Northern Territory, which produced the influential report *Learning Lessons* (Collins, 1999). It concluded that 'many Indigenous students are leaving the school system with the English literacy and numeracy ability of a six to seven-year-old mainstream child', leading to the increased emphasis on literacy and numeracy in the federal sphere (Collins, 1999: 17).

While noting the aims of the original bilingual education programme and applauding some of the outcomes, particularly the employment of indigenous teachers in remote schools and the greater involvement of local communities, the Collins report argued that many schools lacked coherent language practices. It recommended a shift to 'two-way learning', describing it as 'a term which removes the current tendency to see learning in the vernacular and in English as being somehow in competition' (Collins, 1999: 125). In 2000, the Northern Territory introduced a 'Two Way Learning Program' (NTDEET, 2005), with the aim that 'local languages are used primarily as a means of teaching English literacy' (Lugg, 2004, cited in NTDEET, 2005: 28).

In 2000, under new accountability measures, the states and territories were required to assess levels of literacy and numeracy through state-based testing that was benchmarked nationally. The Northern Territory version of this testing was the Multilevel Assessment Program or MAP (NTDEET, 2008), under which the Department of Education, Employment and Training claimed that 'Northern Territory students meet or exceed Australian standards in literacy, numeracy and all learning' (NTDEET, 2008: 5).

In 2005, when the Northern Territory Department of Employment, Education and Training produced the *Indigenous Languages and Culture in NT Schools Report 2004–2005*, only 10 government schools had two-way learning programmes, despite others using unofficial bilingual 'approaches and pedagogies' (NTDEET, 2005: 30). Although in 2004 and 2005 the Northern Territory government committed to revitalising the bilingual education programmes, in practice it was not a priority, as reflected in declining resources for such programmes (NTDEET, 2005, 2006). Furthermore, evidence of systemic approaches to improving levels of literacy and numeracy amongst indigenous children was not apparent (Simpson *et al.*, 2009).

In May 2008, the first national testing programme of literacy and numeracy standards, the NAPLAN (National Assessment Program Literacy and Numeracy), took place (MCEECDYA, 2009). The summary report released later that year displayed the depth of disadvantage and the poor educational outcomes for remote indigenous students (Simpson *et al.*, 2009). The high-stakes literacy and numeracy test allowed for the first time national comparison of student outcomes on literacy and numeracy (NTDET, 2009), and the poor performance of indigenous students across the Northern Territory, particularly in very remote areas, was used as the justification for the effective dismantling of bilingual education programmes, as reported by *Four Corners*.

Planning for the National Curriculum, implemented under the Rudd Labor government in 2008, further strengthened the role of the federal government vis-à-vis the states and territories. Testing is now integral to literacy and numeracy across school levels. However, such policy risks not only being ineffective, but also detrimental. In Marika's (2000: 50) words, policy such as standardised language testing has effects which are 'doubly discriminatory – they ignore Yolnu knowledge and language and they do not reflect the ESL nature of Yolnu students'. The ideological value judgements of mainstream Australian society about the dominant status of English, reflected in policy choices, thus have the potential to threaten the survival of the remaining indigenous languages and culture in remote communities.

Dismantling Bilingual Education

The recent decision to move away from bilingual education was taken in the context of a difficult set of political circumstances facing the Northern Territory government. The government was blamed for the failure of its previous policies directed at indigenous people, including education. In this particular case education issues were conflated with other issues. In 2007 a dramatic and unforeseen emergency intervention into the Northern Territory was announced by the federal government under the leadership of Coalition Prime Minister John Howard. It was in response to the release of the report *Ampe Akelyernemane Meke Mekarle 'Little Children are Sacred'* (Wild & Anderson, 2007), which examined the issue of child sexual abuse in remote indigenous communities. The federal government proclaimed a national emergency in many remote indigenous communities and introduced far-reaching measures to deal with it, overriding the Northern Territory government. Altman and Johns (2008: v) highlight the significance of the intervention: 'this announcement subsequently brought about the most radical legislative and policy shifts seen in the past 30 years in Indigenous affairs'. The measures were race-based; they applied only to indigenous people in the Northern Territory in 'prescribed areas' (Altman & Johns, 2008: v); and they could only be implemented by setting aside the Racial Discrimination Act of 1975.

Five hundred communities were affected across the Northern Territory: in total, more than 40,000 people (Commonwealth of Australia, 2008). Welfare payments were withheld, changes were made to land ownership, and health checks and building works were initiated. The ways in which the measures were imposed on all people within the designated communities aroused deep anger (Commonwealth of Australia, 2008). The intervention was instigated towards the end of the Howard government's 11 years in power, but was animated by beliefs and assumptions articulated and given force in its earlier terms. The Howard years had been characterised by an attempt to reframe Australian history and the role of indigenous people within it. Taken up by conservative commentators, these views began, over time, to be recast as a 'discourse of policy failure', so that policy aimed at indigenous people became shaped by the view that policies of self-determination had failed (Altman *et al.*, 2005: 1). The intervention was based on this premise and played a powerful role in aggregating and positioning indigenous people as 'dysfunctional' (Simpson *et al.*, 2009: 23), thus requiring punitive treatment by the government.

A sea change in Northern Territory politics took place after the federal government's intervention. In the months following, the Chief Minister and the Education Minister resigned (Dewar, 2009). The intervention cast the Northern Territory government as at best incompetent and at worst wilfully negligent, because it had failed to provide even basic services and protection for the most vulnerable indigenous people. At the same time, indigenous people themselves were further stigmatised and subjected to extraordinary measures that left many feeling that their worth as human beings had been significantly diminished (Commonwealth of Australia, 2008). After the change of government federally in 2007, the incoming Rudd government reviewed the intervention and retained elements of it, although with a commitment to reinstating the Racial Discrimination Act and to a more consultative process. A Council of Australian Governments (COAG) meeting in 2008 committed to 'close the gap' between indigenous and non-indigenous Australians, including in education. The achievement of better standards of literacy and numeracy were prioritised (Altman, 2009; Snyder & Nieuwenhuysen, 2010).

In August 2008, the Northern Territory Labor government suffered an electoral reversal when it went to the polls a year early, retaining power by only one seat (Dewar, 2009). Following the release of the NAPLAN data in September, which showed that Northern Territory children had performed poorly in literacy and numeracy tests, the CEO of the Department of Employment, Education and Training, Margaret Banks, resigned (Dewar, 2009). On 13 October 2008, the Report of the Northern Territory Emergency Response Review Board was released by the federal government. It contained a damning indictment of the Northern Territory government in relation to education in remote indigenous communities, describing 'catastrophic education outcomes in remote communities' (Commonwealth of Australia, 2008, n.p.). While the Review Board did not exonerate previous federal governments, it suggested that the Northern Territory Department of Education and Training and governments as a whole had failed to respond adequately over many years. On 14 October, the Minister's imposition of the four hours a day rule was announced (Scrymgour, 2008).

In this context, Minister Scrymgour's directive to schools can be viewed as an attempt to reassert control in an environment where political choices had been circumscribed by new national testing frameworks and the intervention. Reflecting on the impact of the decision, Kral (2009: 3) observes that 'the move to abolish bilingual education has, in effect, given the Indigenous bilingual educators the impression that their program was a failure', despite the apparently successful literacy learning that had occurred. But this ministerial directive did not meet with popular support. The 'backlash' that resulted from the Minister's decision led to some change in the directive, with a commitment that the four hours a day rule 'would be negotiated with each of the Territory's nine bilingual schools on a case-by-case basis' (Robinson, 2008).

Although the Minister's decision could be considered hasty and ill-judged, Simpson et al. (2009: 35) note that 'the debate cannot be cast in simple terms of respect versus lack of respect for Indigenous identity and heritage', partly because the Minister herself was indigenous. Instead, they argue that her decision displayed a lack of understanding of the ways both language and literacy are acquired, which brings us back to where we began in this chapter: the value-laden nature of language and literacy education.

Final Comment

Despite significant setbacks, there is still room for hope. As the history of bilingual education in Australia illustrates, radical changes are not necessarily permanent. Decisions taken by politicians in an atmosphere of crisis are often modified, as has already happened with the four hours a day rule. This reflects not just the reality of indigenous language use in schools, but also the determined resistance of some indigenous communities, such as Yuendumu and Yirrkala. Over the past 30 years there has been some progress in education for indigenous people in remote communities, the vast majority of whom now attend school for at least some of the year, which was not the case in the 1970s (Altman et al., 2004). Moreover, the growing number of trained indigenous teachers and workers in local communities are themselves powerful agents of change. Under current conditions in Australia, we are seeing the rise of English, but in the future we might again see the rise of a pluralistic approach to indigenous education that recognises and respects the importance of local languages and cultures as foundational to educational achievement.

References

ABS (Australian Bureau of Statistics) (2008) Regional statistics, Northern Territory, Cat. 1362.7. Online document, accessed 9 December 2009. http://www.abs.gov.au.

ABS (Australian Bureau of Statistics) (2009) Australian demographic statistics, Cat. 3101.0. Online document, accessed 9 December 2009. http://www.abs.gov.au.

Altman, J.C. (2009) Beyond closing the gap: Valuing diversity in indigenous Australia (Working Paper no. 54). Canberra: Centre for Aboriginal Economic Policy Research, Australian National University. Online document, accessed 6 December 2009. http://www.anu.edu.au/caepr/publications.php.

Altman, J.C. and Johns, M. (2008) Indigenous welfare reform in the Northern Territory and Cape York: A comparative analysis (Working Paper no. 44). Canberra: Centre for Aboriginal Economic Policy Research, Australian National University. Online document, accessed 6 December 2009. http://www.anu.edu.au/caepr/publications.php.

Altman, J.C., Biddle, N. and Hunter, B. (2004) Indigenous socioeconomic change 1971–2001: A historical perspective (Discussion Paper no. 266). Canberra: Centre for Aboriginal Economic Policy Research, Australian National University. Online document, accessed 6 December 2009. http://www.anu.edu.au/caepr/publications.php.

Altman, J.C., Linkhorn, C. and Clarke, J. (2005) Land rights and development reform in remote Australia (Discussion Paper no. 26). Canberra: Centre for Aboriginal Economic Policy Research, Australian National University. Online document, accessed 6 December 2009. http://www.anu.edu.au/caepr/publications.php.

Attwood, B. (2005) *Telling the Truth about Aboriginal History.* Sydney: Allen and Unwin.

Bell, L. and Stevenson, H. (2006) *Education Policy: Process, Themes and Impact.* London: Routledge.

Caffery, J. (2002) Australian indigenous languages: A brief status report. *Ngoonjook,* July, 5–6.

Cahnmann, M. and Varghese, M.M. (2005) Critical advocacy and bilingual education in the United States. *Linguistics and Education* 16, 59–73.

Calma, T. (2009) Your say: Calma responds to bilingual debate. *National Indigenous Times,* (185), 4 September, accessed 19 December 2009. http://www.nit.com.au.

Collins, B. (1999) *Learning Lessons. An Independent Review of Indigenous Education in the Northern Territory.* Darwin: Northern Territory Department of Education. Online document, accessed 10 December 2009. http://www.det.nt.gov.au/__data/assets/pdf_file/0005/7475/learning_lessons_review.pdf.

Commonwealth of Australia (2000) *The National Indigenous English Literacy and Numeracy Strategy.* Canberra. Online document, accessed 19 December 2009. http://www.dest.gov.au/archive/schools/publications/2000/LNS.pdf.

Commonwealth of Australia (2008) *Report of the NTER Review Board.* Canberra. Online document, accessed 10 December 2009. http://www.nterreview.gov.au.

Cummins, J. (1999) Alternative paradigms in bilingual education research: Does theory have a place? *Educational Researcher* 28, 26–41.

Dawkins, J. (1988) *Strengthening Australia's Schools: A Consideration of the Focus and Content of Schooling.* Canberra: Department of Employment, Education and Training, Australian Government Publishing Service.

DEET (Department of Employment, Education and Training) (1989) *National Aboriginal and Torres Strait Islander Education Policy.* Online document, accessed 16 December 2009. http://www.dest.gov.au/archive/schools/indigenous/aep.htm.

Devlin, B. (1999) Bilingual education and the acquisition of English literacy. *Ngoonjook,* December, 103–106.

Devlin, B. (2009) Bilingual education in the Northern Territory: A brief summary of some issues. *Literacy Link,* 7–8 March, accessed 26 November 2009. http://www.acal.edu.au.

Dewar, M. (2009) Northern Territory. July to December 2008, political chronicles. *Australian Journal of Politics and History* 55 (2), 303–309.

Ernst-Slavit, G. (1997) Different words, different worlds: Language use, power and authorized language in a bilingual classroom. *Linguistics and Education* 9, 25–48.

Ford, L. and Klesch, M. (2003) 'It won't matter soon, we'll all be dead': Endangered languages and action research. *Ngoonjook*, July, 27–43.

Ford, M. (1996) Language nests in New Zealand. Implications for the Australian Aboriginal and Torres Strait Islander context. *The Australian Journal of Indigenous Education* 24 (2), 15–19.

Graff, H.J. (1993) Literacy, myths, and legacies: Lessons from the past/thoughts for the future. *Interchange* 24 (3), 271–286.

Graham, B. (1999) Growing into bilingual education: Jottings from the journey. *Ngoonjook*, December, 55–66.

Harris, S. and Devlin, B. (1997) Bilingual programs involving Aboriginal languages in Australia. In J. Cummins and D. Corson (eds) *Encyclopedia of Language and Education, Vol. 5, Bilingual Education* (pp. 1–14). Dordrecht, The Netherlands: Kluwer Academic Publishers.

HRSCATSUA (House of Representatives Standing Committee on Aboriginal and Torres Strait Islander Affairs) (1992) *A Matter of Survival*. Report of the Inquiry into Aboriginal and Torres Strait Islander Language Maintenance, Commonwealth of Australia, Canberra. Online document, accessed 19 December 2009. http://www.austlii.edu.au/au/other/IndigLRes/1992/2/index.html.

Hughes, H. and Hughes, M. (2008) Separatist schooling failure in the NT. *The Australian*, 17 September, accessed 23 December 2009. http://www.theaustralian.com.au/news/separatist-schooling-failure-in-the-nt/story-e6frg73o-1111117503073.

Jaffe, A. (2003) Talk around text: Literacy practices, cultural identity and authority in a Corsican bilingual classroom. *The International Journal of Bilingual Education and Bilingualism* 6 (3), 202–220.

Kral, I. (2009) The literacy question in remote indigenous Australia (CAEPR Topical Issue no. 6). Canberra: Australian National University, Centre for Aboriginal Economic Policy Research. Online document, accessed 16 August 2010. http://www.anu.edu.au/caepr/publications.php.

Kral, I. and Falk, I. (2004) *What Is All That Learning For? Indigenous Adult English Literacy Practices, Training, Community Capacity and Health*. Adelaide: NCVER.

Lo Bianco, J. (2008a) Bilingual education and socio-political issues. In J. Cummins and D. Corson (eds) *Encyclopedia of Language and Education, Vol. 5, Bilingual Education* (2nd edn) (pp. 35–50). Dordrecht, The Netherlands: Kluwer Academic Publishers.

Lo Bianco, J. (2008b) Language policy and education in Australia. In J. Cummins and D. Corson (eds) *Encyclopedia of Language and Education, Vol. 5, Bilingual Education* (2nd edn) (pp. 343–353). Dordrecht, The Netherlands: Kluwer Academic Publishers.

Marika, R. (2000) Milthun latju wana romgu yolnu: Valuing Yolnu knowledge in the education system. *TESOL in Context* 10 (2), 45–52.

May, S. (1998) Language and education rights for indigenous peoples. *Language, Culture and Curriculum* 11 (3), 272–296.

May, S. (2008) Bilingual/immersion education: What the research tells us. In J. Cummins and D. Corson (eds) *Encyclopedia of Language and Education, Vol. 5, Bilingual Education* (2nd edn) (pp. 19–34). Dordrecht, The Netherlands: Kluwer Academic Publishers.

MCEECDYA (Ministerial Council for Education, Early Childhood Development and Youth Affairs) (2008) *Melbourne Declaration on Educational Goals for Young Australians*. Online document, accessed 23 November 2009. http://www.myceecdya.edu.au.

MCEECDYA (Ministerial Council for Education, Early Childhood Development and Youth Affairs) (2009) *Results for 2009 National Assessment Program Literacy and Numeracy (NAPLAN) National Testing.* Online document, accessed 23 November 2009. http://www.myceecdya.edu.au.

Murphy, I. and Vencio, E. (2009) Maintaining two worlds: The relevance of mother tongue in Brazil's Amerindian societies. *International Journal of Bilingual Education and Bilingualism* 12 (4), 387–400.

Nakata, M. (2003) Some thoughts on literacy issues in indigenous contexts. *The Australian Journal of Indigenous Education* 3, 7–15.

NTDEET (Department of Employment, Education and Training) (2005) *Indigenous Languages and Culture in NT Schools Report 2004–2005.* Online document, accessed 26 November 2009. http://www.det.nt.gov.au.

NTDEET (Department of Employment, Education and Training) (2006) *Indigenous Education Strategic Plan 2006–2009.* Northern Territory Government. Online document, accessed 23 November 2009. http://www.det.nt.gov.au.

NTDEET (Department of Employment, Education and Training) (2008) *Annual Report 2007/2008.* Northern Territory Government. Online document, accessed 23 November 2009. http://www.det.nt.gov.au.

NTDET (Department of Education and Training) (2009) *Annual Report 2008–2009.* Northern Territory Government. Online document, accessed 23 November 2009. http://www.det.nt.gov.au.

Purdie, N., Frigo, T., Ozolins, C., Noblett, G., Thieberger, N. and Sharp, J. (2008) *Indigenous Languages Programmes in Australian Schools. A Way Forward.* Canberra: Australian Government and Australian Council for Educational Research. Online document, accessed 23 November 2009. http://www.dest.gov.au/sectors/school_education/publications_resources/profiles/Indigenous+Languages+Programs+in+Australian+Schools+%E2%80%93+A+Way+Forward.htm.

Robinson, N. (2008) Marion Scrymgour backs down on bilingual education plan. *The Australian*, 16 December, accessed 19 December 2009. http://www.theaustralian.com.au.

Schwab, R. (1995) Twenty years of policy recommendations for indigenous education: Overview and research implications (Discussion Paper no. 92). Canberra: Centre for Aboriginal Economic Policy Research, Australian National University. Online document, accessed 6 December 2009. http://www.anu.edu.au/caepr/publications.php.

Scrymgour, M. (2008) Education restructure includes greater emphasis on English. Media release 14 October, accessed 23 November 2009. http://newsroom.nt.gov.au.

Simpson, J., Caffery, J. and McConvell, P. (2009) Gaps in Australia's indigenous language policy: Dismantling bilingual education in the Northern Territory (AIATSIS Discussion Paper Number 24). Online document, accessed 10 December 2009. http://www.aiatsis.gov.au/research/docs/dp/DP24.pdf.

Snyder, I. (2008) *The Literacy Wars: Why Teaching Children to Read and Write in Australia is a Battlefield.* Sydney: Allen and Unwin.

Snyder, I. and Nieuwenhuysen, J. (eds) (2010) *Closing the Gap in Education? Improving Outcomes in Southern World Societies.* Melbourne: Monash University Publishing.

Street, B. (1984) *Literacy in Theory and Practice.* Cambridge: Cambridge University Press.

Street, B. (1997) Hobbesian fears and Galilean struggles: Response to Peter Freebody's 'Assessment as communal versus punitive practice: Six new literacy crises'. *Literacy & Numeracy Studies* 7 (2), 90–96.

The Age (2008) Gillard backs NT education decision. *The Age*, 19 November, accessed 29 December 2009. http://news.theage.com.au/national/gillard-supports-nt-education-decision-20081119-6bdf.html.

Whitmont, D. (2009) Going back to Lajamanu. *Four Corners*. Australian Broadcasting Commission, 14 September, accessed 23 November 2009. http://www.abc.net.au/4corners/content/2009/s2683288.htm.

Wild, R. and Anderson, P. (2007) *Ampe Akelyernemane Meke Mekarle 'Little Children Are Sacred'*. Board of Inquiry into the Protection of Aboriginal Children from Sexual Abuse. Darwin: Northern Territory Government. Online document, accessed 19 December 2009. http://www.inquirysaac.nt.gov.au.

Wilkins, D. (2008) W(h)ither language, culture and education in remote indigenous communities of the Northern Territory? Online document, accessed 23 November 2009. http://www.australianreview.net/digest/2008/10/wilkins.html.

Wolfe, P. (1999) *Settler Colonialism and the Transformation of Anthropology: The Politics and Poetics of an Ethnographic Event*. London and New York: Cassell.

Yunupingu, G. (1998) We know these things to be true. Third Vincent Lingiari Memorial Lecture, 20 August, accessed 23 December 2009. http://www.austlii.edu.au/au/other/IndigLRes/car/1998/2008.html.

4 (Re)Writing English: Putting English in Translation

Bruce Horner and Min-Zhan Lu

Introduction

In this chapter we examine ways to rethink post-secondary writing instruction for 'L1' as well as 'L2' speakers of English in light of changes to our understanding of English as a medium. While the plural and fluctuating character of English documented by research on world Englishes and on uses of English as a Lingua Franca (hereafter, 'ELF') has prompted serious challenges to programs of language instruction that treat English as a uniform and static set of forms, much of the attention of this research is directed at English instruction outside the Kachruvian 'inner circle' of the Anglo-American sphere (as illustrated by some of the chapters in this volume), or at English instruction for new arrivals to that circle (Rubdy & Saraceni, 2006). For example, Andy Kirkpatrick (2007: 2) describes his book *World Englishes: Implications for International Communication and English Language Teaching* as aimed 'primarily at ELT professionals and trainee teachers undertaking TESOL training throughout the world', and he emphasizes that English language curricula based on a text like his 'should comprise the cultures of the people using the language for cross-cultural communication, rather than Anglo-American cultures' (2007: 3).

While understandable, this focus on English language instruction outside the Anglo-American sphere has eclipsed attention to the implications of this research for the teaching of English within that powerful 'inner' sphere, including curricula intended for those assumed to be 'L1' speakers of English. This eclipse leaves unchallenged the cultural as well as geopolitical base of the ideology of English Only, an ideology whose tenets research on world Englishes and ELF has shown to be invalid. Those tenets treat English as a uniform and static code, the mastery and preservation of which are linked indelibly to social identity and to individual, national and global economic well-being. So long as that ideology dominates language instruction in the 'inner circle', it is likely to dominate language instruction outside that realm as well.

Composition Studies

Our own field of composition studies exemplifies the dominance of this ideology. Composition studies is a field indigenous, and largely restricted, to the United States, arising out of, maintaining, and investigating writing instruction required of virtually all undergraduate students who enroll in US colleges and universities. Manifestations of the dominance of English Only ideology in composition instruction in the US include the assumptions that English will be the sole language of instruction, writing and assigned readings for writing courses; that the aim of such instruction is to enable students to produce a particular, and fixed, variety of English – namely, Standard Written English, or SWE; that all students are native-speakers of English only (Matsuda, 2006; Shuck, 2006); and that students' ability to produce SWE is a primary factor in determining their individual economic well-being as well as the economic well-being of the nation (Horner & Trimbur, 2002). According to this ideology, the role of composition instruction (as well as of language instruction generally) is to enable students to reproduce a static set of language conventions, thought to be codified in SWE, as a means of preparing them to participate fully in the civic and economic life of the nation. These assumptions are so deep-rooted as to seem simply commonsensical; for many in the US, 'writing' means, and means only, writing in English – presumably, SWE – hence teaching writing means teaching SWE.

The broad reach of US composition instruction, in tandem with the hegemonic relation of the US to other nations, positions the teaching of composition in the US to play a significant role in either sustaining or contesting English Only ideology and its sway not just nationally but globally (Lu, 2004). Consequently, it behooves us to examine the implications of research destabilizing the universality, 'purity' and the fixed character of English as a medium for composition instruction in the US, as well as corollary instruction elsewhere. However, the ideological character of English Only means that such examinations are insufficient by themselves to effectively contest its tenets. As Bourdieu (1991: 51) has observed,

> recognition of the legitimacy of the official language has nothing in common with an explicitly professed, deliberate and revocable belief, or

with an intentional act of accepting a 'norm'. It is inscribed, in a practical state, in dispositions which are impalpably inculcated, through a long and slow process of acquisition, by the sanctions of the linguistic market.

Composition instruction, like language instruction generally, certainly contributes to the inculcation of such dispositions – not through simple professions of the tenets of English Only but more discreetly in what its practices treat as ordinary. Consequently, it is only by significant changes to instructional practices that alternative dispositions can be learned, through challenges to the ordinary, albeit culturally produced, responses and actions of students and teachers in their reading and writing.

Research on ELF and World Englishes has identified specific dispositions on which we might draw in rethinking English composition instruction. In reviewing that research here, we distinguish between scholarship on ELF and World Englishes that, paradoxically, appears to reinforce particular tenets of monolingual ideology, and that which offers radical challenges to those tenets. The latter, we argue, has the potential to encourage what we have elsewhere called a translingual approach to language (Horner *et al.*, 2011). Such an approach treats all reading and writing as involving translation across languages, discourses and forms of language, and highlights the necessity of the contribution of writers' and readers' concrete labor to the production of meaning and the maintenance and transformation of specific language practices. Using our analysis of ELF and World Englishes scholarship, we delineate principles by which we believe an 'English' composition pedagogy encouraging a translingual approach and contesting 'English Only' ideology might best be guided, and illustrate how these might be enacted in composition instruction. But while the immediate concern in this chapter is with composition instruction, this discussion might also provoke the development of comparable pedagogies in other areas of language instruction concerned with 'English'.

ELF, World Englishes and English Only Ideology

Scholarship on ELF and on World Englishes is distinct but with significant points of intersection. ELF scholarship is concerned with uses of English in conversations among interlocutors for none of whom English is a first or native language and who share no other language in common, often in settings outside the speakers' region of affiliation – for example, a conversation in English taking place in Seoul between two speakers, one a native Brazilian speaker of Portuguese and one a native Hong Kong speaker of Cantonese.

World Englishes scholarship is concerned with the development and shared use of indigenous varieties of English – for example, Nigerian English, Indian English, China English and Australian English. Despite these differences, both ELF and World Englishes scholarship demonstrate the diversity in Englishes, the legitimacy of these, their susceptibility to change by language users and (hence) the fluidity of their boundaries. Explicitly and implicitly, scholarship on ELF and World Englishes thus has the potential to counter tenets of English Only ideology by

- calling into question reifications of English and of social identity;
- highlighting the agency of language users in communication;
- emphasizing the contributions of language users' labor to the production of meaning and linguistic forms.

The findings of this scholarship demonstrate first and foremost the ideological basis of the continuing power of 'English Only' in language education. Definitions of 'standard' English have been shown to be at best circular (Coupland, 2000), and common distinctions between languages, language circles, native and non-native speakers, and language varieties as fixed and independent entities have failed to hold up under scrutiny (Gal & Irvine, 1995; Kramsch, 1998; Nayar, 1997; Pennycook, 2008). Efforts to impose what are imagined to be English as Native Language (ENL) standards on others have been shown to be both inaccurate in their representations of uses of English even within the Kachruvian inner circle (Kramsch, 1998), and ineffective, even irrelevant, to the communication needs of the majority of users of English (Seidlhofer, 2004).

Admittedly, there are strands of alignment as well as contradiction that have emerged between thinking about ELF and English Only ideology. There is, of course, one strand in explicit arguments for English Only in the US heralding English as the current de facto global lingua franca. This strand, while appearing to sever the ideological link between nationality and language, does so by extending the reach of a standardized view of English associated with the Anglo-American sphere globally. In this version, standardized (Anglo-American) English – aka 'native-speaker' English, or 'ENL' – already is the lingua franca affording efficiency in the global communication of goods, services and knowledge. Other versions of English, significantly including versions of English within the Anglo-American sphere associated with subordinate groups, such as African American English, as well as World Englishes such as China English (Hu, 2004) are viewed as threats to both the integrity of English and the efficiency of the global communication it is believed English otherwise promises to provide. According to this strand, the task of writing instruction is to enable students to produce SWE to achieve and maintain such efficiency.

While most ELF scholars reject treating standardized Anglo-American English as the norm for all users of English to emulate, there are nonetheless significant intersections between the assumptions about language informing some strands of ELF scholarship and arguments for Standardized English as the global lingua franca. Here we distinguish between, on the one hand, definitions of ELF as a core of codified practices alternative to the English promoted in English Only ideology (see, e.g. Jenkins, 2002: 96ff.; Mauranen, 2003: 516–519; Seidlhofer, 2004: 215) and, on the other hand, definitions of ELF that radically challenge notions of language that such cores, and the attempts to identify them, represent. Pennycook (2008: 40) critiques the first version of ELF scholarship when he complains that '[b]y attempting to describe what is common to communication among non-native speakers of English, the ELF approach aims at the re-creation of a different core, decentred from the former loci of correctness but re-centred in new canons of intelligible usage'. Citing scholarship on ELF by Jenkins and Seidlhofer, he notes (2008: 38–39) that the focus of much of this scholarship is on 'form rather than meaning' and is directed at identifying 'a core to English that is more or less stable'. But if, as Rubdy and Saraceni (2006: 10) have observed, such a codified ELF is taken 'as a model for teaching and learning ... the question that arises is whether one form of prescription is not being (unwittingly or even wittingly) replaced by another'.

There is sharp debate on whether this is an accurate interpretation of ELF scholarship, a debate hinging on whether ELF is conceived as a specific linguistic variety whose features are thus subject to codification, for whatever purpose, or rather as a specific function of language use irrespective of such matters as phonology, syntax or lexicon (see Friedrich & Matsuda, 2010). For example, both Seidlhofer (2006) and Jenkins (2006: 161) reject as misconceptions the claims that their scholarship is directed toward a monolithic definition of ELF to be prescribed for use. Nonetheless, we would argue that their efforts are committed to a view of ELF as a specific language variety. The codification of ELF, they argue, is necessary as a step toward the acceptance of this variety rather than its dismissal as a substandard use of English. For example, Seidlhofer, citing Bamgbose's argument (1998: 5) that 'as long as non-native English norms remain uncodified, they cannot become a point of reference for usage and acceptance', asserts that 'you need to be able to *show* what it is you want people to accept' (Seidlhofer, 2006: 43). ELF is thus offered as a distinct variety to be accepted, and used, in those contexts in which it serves as a common language for speakers none of whom know it as their 'mother' tongue (Jenkins, 2006: 160). What it offers, in such contexts, is a set of 'certain forms (phonological, lexicogrammatical, etc.) that are widely used and widely intelligible across groups of English speakers from different first language backgrounds' (Jenkins, 2006: 161).

Such arguments call for toleration of difference. At the same time, however, they retain a notion of language varieties as fairly discrete entities each of which consists of a set of forms 'appropriate' to a specific context. In this sense, this strand of ELF scholarship is in alignment with strands of scholarship on World Englishes that likewise forward codifications of specific World Englishes each of which is associated with a specific population and/or geographic region – Indian English, Australian English, Nigerian English, and so on (see, e.g. Arua, 1998; Delbridge, 1999; Hay *et al.*, 2008; Hu, 2004; Kirkpatrick & Zhichang, 2002; Shim, 1999). Pursuit of this strategy of language pluralization, however, risks retaining and thus supporting monolingualist beliefs in languages as stable, internally uniform, discrete sets of forms and practices tied to social (national or regional) identities, likewise treated as stable, uniform and discrete. Thus, for example, whatever the intentions of the scholars engaged in the identification of an ELF core, that pursuit puts their work in close alignment with the reification of language obtaining in English Only arguments that emphasize its standardization, imagined to be codified in SWE. This is especially troublesome in the context of current geopolitical relations making English Only ideology prevalent. Likewise, as Canagarajah (2007: 929) has observed, the model of communication informing the emphasis in this scholarship on 'intelligibility' is in alignment with the valorization of efficiency of communication in English Only ideology, and its assumption of the necessity of a standardized language practice to achieve that efficiency. By identifying communication with use of particular forms of language, ELF scholars' valorization of efficiency obscures both the possibility of diverse meanings and the necessity of language users' concrete labor in the struggle over and production of meaning. This is pedagogically troubling insofar as it denies language users' agency as contributors to meaning production through their labor. Rather than being granted a role in the production of meaning through their work *with* language, users are reduced to the role of simply exchanging, efficiently or not, meanings posited as already extant in language, through use of the appropriate code. The model of the writer implied here is of someone writing 'in' a language, and its code, or failing to, rather than writing, and rewriting, the language in each instance of writing.

Finally, identifying an ELF 'core' supports a transmission model of pedagogy that has long been held suspect for appearing to maintain asymmetrical power relations between teacher and student.[1] Seidlhofer herself has explicitly rejected the kind of prescriptivist pedagogy that would seem to exemplify such power relations, asserting that 'it is not my task, and indeed impossible, to pre-empt any local pedagogic decisions', and explaining that transmitting the findings on intelligibility in ELF to ELF users 'is not a matter of imposing a norm, . . . but of offering an alternative possibility' (2006: 45). Jenkins calls for a pedagogy aimed at teaching 'about Englishes, their similarities and differences, issues involved in intelligibility, the strong link between language and identity, and so on' through 'exposure to a range of W[orld E[nglishe]s and ELF varieties, [. . .] includ[ing] discussion of the reasons for the spread of English, the development of diverse standards, the relationship between language and identity, and the like' (2006: 173, 174). But such pedagogies risk effectively adopting a 'laissez-faire' policy that, like the tacit policy of English Only dominating the US currently, cedes to existing power relations and dominant ideology the determination of the rules to be followed in a particular context. In short, while it would seem a good thing for students to be aware of variation in uses of English, a pedagogy stipulating the existence of codified varieties in advance might well work against students' sense of agency in varying (or, for that matter, replicating) specific forms in their language use. For the focus in such a pedagogy would remain on the varieties themselves rather than their users.[2]

Despite the apparent alignments outlined above between some strands of ELF scholarship and English Only ideology dominating university writing instruction in the Anglo-American sphere, other strands of scholarship on ELF and World Englishes pose radical challenges to that ideology. As Canagarajah (2007: 937, n. 6) has noted, it is possible to distinguish between those ELF scholars 'on the quest to define [ELF] according to an identifiable grammatical and phonological system' and 'an alternate school that focuses on the pragmatic features that enable [ELF] communication'.[3] We would include in this 'alternate school' those strands of scholarship that, rather than focusing on the identification of a universal core of features to ELF, highlight the strategies by which L2 users of English communicate with other L2 users of English in circumstances where no other language is shared (Meierkord, 2004: 112). Among the most interesting findings of this research has been that '[ELF] is intersubjectively constructed in each specific context of interaction . . . negotiated by each set of speakers for their purposes' and thus 'never achieves a stable or even standardized form' (Meierkord, 2004: 129, quoted in Canagarajah, 2007: 925). And not just the forms ELF takes, but 'even the enabling pragmatic strategies do not have to be the same' for its speakers (Canagarajah, 2007: 926). Thus, while it might be possible to abstract and teach a grammar and lexicon from a particular instance of ELF, that very abstraction would work against students' ability to participate meaningfully in the multilingual languaging that continually re-constitutes

ELF. As Sifakis (2006: 155) has put it, '[V]ariability in the communication between different NNSs renders any attempt at codifying the various uses of English in [ELF] situations difficult, since we would have to know in advance many things that are situation-specific and user-dependent'. Further, because ELF is reconstituted in each instance of its practice, we cannot identify a particular set of practices with 'competence' in it. Instead, as House (2003) states, '[A] lingua franca speaker is not per definitionem not fully competent in the part of his or her linguistic knowledge under study', a point Canagarajah (2007: 925) reiterates: 'all users of [ELF] have native competence of [ELF]'.[4] Thus, teachers can assume neither the need to move students toward a state of 'competence' in ELF nor the stability of that state itself.

There is a significant parallel here between these challenges to teachers of ELF and the challenges faced by teachers of SWE in ostensibly L1 settings. The hope that students can be equipped with a standardized ELF is at odds with the actual multilingual practices in which language users engage ELF. Likewise, analyses of academic literacy practices in English have shown that the kind of writing taught in the first-year university writing courses most students in US post-secondary schools are required to take is neither applicable to nor of much value in the kinds of writing practiced in the disciplines and in the workplace (see Petraglia, 1995). Analyses of academic literacy practices in the United Kingdom (see Lea & Street, 1998) show a similar lack of uniformity in expectations for writing, instructors' beliefs to the contrary notwithstanding.

There are two alternative responses to these findings. The first follows an archipelago model of language and instruction, whereby diverse sets of language practices, imagined as reified and discrete, are codified for transmission to students: core ELF for Non-Native Speakers (NNSs), standardized Anglo-American English for residents of the Kachruvian inner circle, chemistry writing for the chemists, business writing for the business majors. Each is imagined as 'appropriate' to a particular site, discipline or occasion. This archipelago response trades in reification of one standard as universal for a host of separate reifications, each allowed its appropriate place in a hierarchy of languages – vernacular vs standard, or spoken vs written English, say, or academic vs non-academic, or formal vs informal. Lea and Street have identified such a response as an 'academic socialization' approach to teaching academic literacy, which they characterize as 'concerned with students' acculturation into disciplinary and subject-based discourses and genres .... *[treated as] relatively stable'* (2006: 369, emphasis added). As Lillis and Scott (2007) observe, this 'academic socialization' approach responds to the documented plurality of academic literac-ies (sic) by treating these varieties as normative. It responds to the plurality of academic literacies by aiming to 'identify and induct': 'identifying academic conventions ... [and] exploring how students might be taught to become proficient or "expert" in them' (Lillis & Scott, 2007: 13). Thus, while the academic 'socialization' model grants legitimacy to different varieties of language, it reinforces, by understating, the role of existing power relations in determining what may or may not show 'competence' in using language 'appropriate' to a given situation, and according to what and whose interests a particular practice is deemed 'appropriate' (Dubin, 1989; Fairclough, 1992; Leung, 2005: 131–132; McKay, 2003). A place for every language, or form of writing, and every language and form of writing kept to its place, with the politics of determining what is and is not appropriate to that site or occasion sidestepped through invocation of 'appropriateness'.[5] The possibility of promoting interaction between varieties in ways that 'transform' them – a term invoked by Lillis and Scott (2007) in their summary of the 'academic literacies' perspective – is not considered; instead, each variety is treated as stable (see Kramsch's warning, 2006: 103). Thus, despite the 'archipelago' and the 'academic socialization' perspectives' recognition of the plurality of academic literac-ies, these themselves are treated as largely autonomous rather than, in Street's sense, ideological: operating autonomously on writers and readers to produce specific, determined effects (Street, 1984). Occluded in such accounts of academic literacy/ies is the agency of writers and readers exercised through their practices with literacy/ies. Literacies, and by extension languages, are treated as tools to be picked up and used; specific contexts for these tools are identified, and the uses of the tools for these contexts are then explained. In this model, as Pennycook (2010: 8) observes, language remains abstracted from practice.

A further problem with the archipelago model arises in its encounter with what various writers have identified as 'traffic' (Kramsch, 2006; Pennycook, 2008). First, there is the traffic of humans from site to site, community to community; second, there is the traffic in meanings among these; and finally, there is the traffic in linguistic forms used. To put it more concretely, diverse language practices, identities and users, far from remaining discrete and fixed, mix and intermingle in ways unseemly to those attempting to codify and maintain particular practices in language, including writing practices, to the point that teaching the 'core' appropriate to any one site misleads (cf. Leung, 2005: 132).

Current debate on World Englishes illustrates this dilemma. On the one hand, the documentation of competing versions of 'English' worldwide has the potential to pose a radical challenge to the notion of a single, uniform ('inner circle') English to be imposed globally. At the same time, the codifications of these competing versions can lead to treatment of them as normative.

Occluding the fluctuating and permeable character of these versions themselves and the agency of those deploying them, there is acceptance of problematic reifications of particular varieties of English tied to particular national identities (e.g. 'China English', 'Australian English', etc. – see Delbridge, 1999; Hu, 2004; Kirkpatrick & Zhichang, 2002). This elides the subjection of all such versions to change and interaction with other languages and language varieties and the politics of standardizing them (Parakrama, 1995; Pennycook, 2003: 516–522).

The second, alternative, response to recognition of the absence of a set of stable core language forms views language pedagogy as a site for both critical analysis and transformation of language practices rather than as the occasion for transmitting such a core, or set of cores. As Lea and Street (1998: 158) observe, whereas commonly 'the codes and conventions of academia [are] taken as givens', an 'academic literacies' approach to understanding 'what it means to become academically literate' requires that we not make 'prior assumptions as to which practices are either appropriate or effective'. In this alternative response, languages, literacies and contexts are treated not as givens but rather as the ongoing product of social action, that is, as practices (Pennycook, 2010: 8). Indeed, Lillis and Scott (2007: 12–13) identify the 'academic literacies' approach with the aim of being explicitly transformative of literacy practices. To adopt this 'practices' approach thus problematizes, contests and holds the potential for transformation of not only the conventions identified with specific practices but the practices themselves. Those taking this response view the scene of instruction for English writing as a site and resource for investigating, with students, strategies by which English may be rewritten, to what effects and under what circumstances, and to training in the development of such strategies and the attitudes that would sustain them.[6]

Adopting such a view of language education would involve a shift from treating as the norm not what Caribbean writers Jean Bernabé, Patrick Chamoiseau and Raphaël Confiant (1989; Pennycook, 2008: 37–38) term mere tolerance for linguistic *diversité* but *diversalité* and *créolité*; not codeswitching but code-meshing; not a pluralizing of discrete varieties of language but a mixing of these, combined with a critique of the use of invocations of appropriateness to establish suspect norms for language use at any given site or occasion (Fairclough, 1992). This involves no longer thinking of English, or a practice with it (or any other language), as operating discrete from other languages or language practices but always 'in translation', negotiating difference and boundaries (Pennycook, 2008: 41). And consequently, it means no longer designing the teaching of English in terms of transmitting either a single set of codified forms, or a host of such sets, but instead, as inculcating dispositions towards and critically engaged, potentially transformative practices with these. Far from being aimed at assisting students only in specialized communicative situations, or at assisting only 'special' students, teaching of such dispositions would in fact be useful in preparing all students for a plethora of communicative situations insofar as the monolingualist norm is in fact chimerical: if English is always a language in translation, then even interlocutors in ostensibly 'ordinary', monolingual situations engage in 'translation' to produce meaning.

Pedagogies for Re-writing English

It is a testament to the power of English Only ideology (and, more broadly, its monolingual equivalents) that pedagogical models of English instruction aimed at code transmission dominate despite their contradiction by language practices on the ground. Nonetheless, models pursuing alternatives are being developed. In the remainder of this chapter we identify the key principles and features of these models and ways these might be implemented in the teaching of writing, including teaching writing to English monolinguals.[7]

Briefly, these are as follows:

- the fluidity, hybridity and performed character of language and identity;
- the agency of writers to deploy language resources;
- writing/reading as the production of and struggle over meaning, rather than 'communication' of pre-existing meanings, clearly or not;
- shifts in the stance and strategies to be taught readers/writers to tolerance, patience, humility, cooperation, accommodation and negotiation;
- emphasis on fluency in working with, rather than within, languages.

As we have already suggested, to be effective, pedagogical strategies following these principles and features must intervene in 'dispositions' deeply inscribed in and held by both teachers and students. And as we discuss below, adapting strategies scholars have identified with oral ELF practices to writing involves addressing reading and writing together as a process in which readers and writers negotiate over meaning as well as changing trained English Only dispositions to reject alternative forms as simply 'wrong'. That is to say, these strategies will work on, and against, dominant cultural dispositions, especially challenging for those identifying themselves as native English speakers because of the high status associated with ENL. Finally, they will focus on practices rather than forms, except insofar as these forms can be understood in terms of practices. That is to say, whether the forms a writer deploys are recognized as conventional or not, the concern will be with what the production of these might accomplish as social action. As Horner *et al.* (2011, 304–305) argue regarding a translingual approach, such an approach will 'ask what produces the appearance of conformity, as well as what that might and might not do, for whom, and how ... not whether [a text's] language is standard, but what the writers are doing with language, and why'.[8]

The most common contemporary strategy in writing instruction for emphasizing the fluidity, hybridity and performed character of language and identity, and the agency of writers to deploy language resources, is to introduce students to examples of apparently deviant texts: the writings of Gloria Anzaldúa or Haunani-Kay Trask, for example, both of which include mixtures of English and other languages, or writings of African Americans which include representations of African American Vernacular English. When granted the imprimatur of being assigned readings, these challenge both canonical notions of the norm for SWE and the identification of SWE with particular social identities. However, by itself this strategy may also risk reinforcing the canonical status of writing by writers not already marked as racial and/or linguistic others in the social imaginary. To prevent this, we might engage students in identifying the linguistically hybrid character of texts already enjoying canonical status, authored by those who seem to exemplify the national or universal 'norm'. For example, in the US teachers and students might investigate the use of mixtures of snatches of song, Latin and verse with highly formal as well as vernacular expressions in *Walden* (1995), that canonical text by dead, white, male American author Henry David Thoreau.[9] Here, as Lu (1999) has observed, it would be crucial not to treat these mixtures as evidence of the 'special' status of the authors as 'creative' or 'geniuses' but as indeed the 'norm' for all writers. Etymological investigation of texts can help with this by revealing the 'mongrel' character of all writings of English, and examination of canonical texts from different historical periods can reveal the radically varying character of what has been deemed 'standard' written English.

Grasping the fluidity of such standards can shift students' sense that writing is an exercise in reproducing 'correct' forms to a sense that writing involves drawing on all one's various linguistic resources for particular ends, and of negotiating the meaning of the resources deployed with readers.[10] This replaces the dominant, but problematic, approach of locating 'power' and 'agency' in particular linguistic forms for teachers to then 'give' to students to use in prescribed ways (Gore, 1992; Luke, 1998) with an approach that helps students to recognize their own agency and power as language users to put language to various uses. To revise Widdowson's formulation, we can have students learn to recognize English as something they 'own' in the sense that it is theirs to write, or re-write – by working on and with it – rather than something already extant which they are to write 'in'.

To ensure that students come to recognize their 'ownership' of English rather than assuming that such ownership belongs only to published authors, we can work with our students to grasp the logic of non-idiomatic phrasings in their own writing and to resist the temptation to dismiss the writing of others that deviates from their expectations as simply 'wrong'. This is different from misleading students into thinking anything goes, or that they are all-powerful as writers. Instead it is to grant them some agency as writers in conjunction with the agency of others, such as readers, and thus to highlight writing and reading as a process of producing and struggling over meanings. Useful in imagining what this entails is Pennycook's (2008: 43) notion of English as a language always in translation, with its emphasis on semio-diversity and the charge to language educators of increasing 'the breadth of meanings available within a language'. We take Pennycook's notion of English as a language always in translation as a reminder that rather than valorizing clarity and efficiency in communication above all, we need to highlight the inevitability of ambiguities in language meaning. This has the pedagogical advantage of transforming students' experience of confusion in their reading and writing from being viewed by them, and their teachers, as failings they should hide into being viewed as resources they can explicitly address to better grasp and make productive use of.

Useful as well to imagining what is entailed in granting students some agency are the insights of research on ELF in practice that highlight the strategies by which meanings are negotiated (see Seidlhofer, 2004: 218 for a summary of these). These insights direct us to encourage in our students the attitudes and strategies, or strategies equivalent to, those found among prac-titioners of spoken ELF in making use of such semiodiversity. Together, these encourage non-dominant, but nonetheless valuable, 'dispositions' in readers and writers of tolerance, patience, humility, cooperation, accommodation and negotiation. The goal here would be to replace attempts to produce the 'ability to speak and write according to the rules of the academy and the social etiquette of one social group' with not just 'the adaptability to select those forms of accuracy and those forms of appropriateness that are called for in a given social context of use', as has been proposed (Kramsch, 1998: 27), but also, as Lillis and Scott (2007: 12–13) suggest, the ability to trans-form those forms and those contexts by questioning the politics of determin-ing appropriateness (see also Canagarajah, 2006).

To illustrate these possibilities we turn to the experience one of us had discussing a set of writings by a student (hereafter, Writer M.) written for a composition course required of all first-year students at our university.[11] These writings included the construction 'can able to'. From an 'English Only' perspective, this construction would be simply an 'error', particularly in light of the fact that Writer M. was a Chinese Non-Native English Speaking (NNES) student from Malaysia and (therefore) someone who lacked authorization to use English in unconventional ways and whose competence in producing SWE was suspect. And in fact, this was the perspective English monolingual students discussing Writer M.'s writing were initially disposed to adopt. They stated that 'can able to' was a clear case of a 'foreign' speaker making an 'error' when trying to use English. As they explained, the word 'can' in idiomatic English is synonymous with 'able to', and hence 'can able to' was redundant.

The instructor then drew the students' attention to Writer M.'s use of 'can' and 'may' in conventional ways elsewhere in her writings: for example, 'she can feel the strong bond with land her people have which the "haole" could not feel'; 'I can say that these are the "obstacles" to success'; 'I may conclude that this particular student has climbed his first step to become a "critical thinker"'. The instructor drew students' attention to such uses of 'can' and 'may' to counter the view that the 'can able to' construction represented an inefficient, because incorrect, use of standardized English 'code', and to encourage students to view their experience of the ambiguity of its meaning to be 'the norm' and a norm calling not for dismissal but for their labor as readers in producing meaning – labor best accomplished through the adoption of attitudes of tolerance, patience, humility, cooperation and accommodation, and through negotiation with the writing and a questioning perspective on idiomaticity. In line with this counterview, the instructor and the students explored possible reasons for the writer to coin the phrase 'can able to' (rather than dismissing this as simply wrong). This led to the discovery that Writer M. consistently used 'can' by itself in relation to a person's will and aptitude not requiring external permission: for example, 'she *can* feel the strong bond with land her people have which the "haole" *could* not feel'. Yet, in the opening statement in that segment, M. wrote: 'As a Hawaiian native historian, Trask *can able to* argue for her people'. This latter statement suggests that Trask's ability to argue for her people is the result not only of her will and capability as a native but also of her having gained permission to do so from her Western audience as a result of her academic qualifications.

By paying attention to these differences in the ways in which the student writer opted for the term 'can' and 'can able to', students in the course developed a sensitivity to the relationship between individual ability and the material conditions in which that ability may be realized, and to the ways in which the idiomatic use of 'can' and 'be able to' in North America occludes attention to that relation. That relation was one Writer M. had argued was significant for English users such as the Hawaiian historian Trask, whose writing the students were analyzing, and Writer M. herself, given her account of her experience as a female member of her family in Malaysia. In short, the English monolingual students began to acknowledge some of the reasoning motivating Writer M.'s use of a non-idiomatic construction. And in fact, when asked to talk about what she was aiming to do with 'can able to', Writer M. explained that 'can' has the additional meaning of 'having permission to', as does the term 'may' in idiomatic English, that is not repre-sented by the phrase 'be able to' alone. To capture a sense of both ability and permission, Writer M. formed 'can able to', as when, referring to college coursework encouraging students to consider different views, she wrote, 'If a student can able to approach each situation with different perspectives than the one he brought from high school, I may conclude that this particu-lar student has climbed his first step to become a "critical thinker"'.

In performing the kind of 'close' analysis of Writer M.'s papers which is traditionally applied only to the work of canonical, published writers, the English monolingual students discovered two ways of accounting for their original dismissal of 'can able to' as an error: (1) the dominant American belief in the transcendental power of the individual, a belief Writer M. expected her readers to bring to her text and one she hoped to disrupt, and (2) English Only ideology. Further, they came to see that to simply 'correct' 'can able to' by changing it to 'can' would require conformity not just to idiomatic ENL but also to English Only ideology and to the dominant US cultural belief in the power of the individual. And they recognized not only that the standardized rules of English could not articulate experiences central to Writer M.'s existence, but also that students like themselves as well as Writer M. can able to work with English in ways that will effectively arti-culate and legitimate, as well as rethink, experiences and beliefs.

Another of our own attempts to work with English in these ways involved asking mostly English monolingual students to investigate an example of an ostensibly 'erroneous' English translation that has garnered a great deal of internet attention: the Chinese restaurant menu item 'Every form rape' ('May I Take Your Order').[12] When analyzing over 700 postings on a website in response to this example of 'Chinglish', students noticed that in spite of the heated discussion in the postings over whether one is to laugh 'at' or 'with' the owner's and/or translator's English, almost all of those who posted responses assumed that the word 'rape' can only mean sexual assault. The writers of the posts thus saw the translation as a humorous result of the translator's lack of proper training in SWE. Only two out of the 720 postings indicated knowledge that 'rape' can also mean a form of vegetable, a meaning none of the students in the class had been aware of prior to reading those two postings.

This led the class to share a series of findings illustrating the peculiarity of students' own 'native' ignorance of rape as a vegetable. These findings included the creation of the commercial label 'Canola' by a Canadian company to promote oil from cold-pressed rape by breaking the association of 'rape' with sexual assault and with a tradition of industrial and military uses for rapeseed oil. Students reported that 'canola', unlike 'rape', was a common term in their vocabulary for food items. This finding also pointed to the conditions of possibility making the vegetable meaning of the term 'rape' fairly common knowledge among Chinese users of English. These conditions have included the following: (1) rape is a popular vegetable in Chinese cooking; (2) China is the biggest producer of rapeseed (17%) (Wikipedia); (3) for Chinese people over 40 who had English classes in school, 'rape' was one of the first English words their textbook introduced them to, along with the terms 'rice', 'wheat', 'maize', 'hammer', 'shovel' and the slogan, 'Workers and farmers are the masters of our motherland.' Such findings made the US culture's reduction of the uses of the word *rape* to refer to sexual assault seem peculiar. It also helped students to consider the specific conditions and relations of life sustaining use of the word as a form of vegetable and part of the logic of a translation that has appeared ludicrous to most English monolinguals residing in the inner circle.

Engaging students in re-reading and rethinking uses of English that at first glance appear to be simply 'wrong' inevitably highlights the restrictions that conformity to English Only ideology places on the kinds of meanings that might be produced, but also the cultural material conditions out of which both 'idiomatic' and 'non-idiomatic' uses arise, as well as the ways in which such conditions might be contested through particular practices with English (see Kramsch, 1998: 29–30). But more importantly, such engagement increases fluency in dispositions opposed to English Only: dispositions of tolerance, humility, patience and a willingness to engage in cooperation, accommodation and negotiation. Further, it involves recognizing that rewriting English, vs learning to write 'in' 'English', is an ongoing process, for both teachers and students, of learning and doing, of participating in language as living 'constitutive activity', what Raymond Williams has called 'a persistent kind of creation and re-creation ... a constant regenerative process' (1977: 31–32). The concept of fluent mastery of a language is inapplicable to language defined thus as subject to constant re-invention. In this sense, ELF users' additional strategy of letting ambiguities pass is fully appropriate and, concretely, the norm in interactions, both written and spoken, where the aim is not to produce particular utterances in conformity to putative standards constituting 'ENL' but to sustain and develop the process of discoursing.

Of course, language use understood as negotiation and translation is by definition always fraught with possibilities for miscommunication, misunderstanding and failure, as well as cooperation, edification and communion. But however frustrating to those pursuing 'efficiency' in teaching and in language use, this is the norm not only in those communicative situations where negotiation and translation are more recognizable but in more 'ordinary' communicative situations as well. Any communicative situation carries the potential for frustration, but also possibilities for change and insight, for writers, readers and the culture(s) they participate in (re)constructing through their reading and writing. In this sense, asking students to rewrite English is simply asking them to do what all of them must always do and have always done in their ordinary work as language users, in contradiction to what dominant ideological beliefs about language would have us believe. In their writing in English, students (inevitably) re-write English, and in so doing, they put English in (cultural) translation, with all the difficulties and delights that such work entails. We can help explore these by joining them in that work.[13]

Notes

(1) See for example Freire (1970). There is a longstanding debate (Bartlett, 2009; Bizzell, 1991; Burbules, 1986; Gore, 1992; Lu & Horner, 1998; A. Luke, 1998; C. Luke, 1996; Miller, 1998) regarding power and teacher authority in 'critical' pedagogies.

(2) See, for example, Kubota's (2001) account of a course aimed at teaching World Englishes to US Native English Speaker (NES) students.

(3) Canagarajah (2007: 937, n. 7) identifies Jenkins and Seidlhofer with the first group and identifies House, Meierkord and himself with the 'alternate' school. While drawing on that distinction here, we recognize that it does not fully represent the work of these and other individual scholars, which tends in specific ways to cross these (and other) categorizations.

(4) Canagarajah (2007: 937, n. 2) acknowledges that he is using 'LFE' ('Lingua Franca English') to refer to what other scholars identify as ELF.

(5) The key document in composition studies representative of this is the Conference on College Composition and Communication position statement 'Students' Right to Their Own Language' (Horner, 2001).

(6) Cf. Burgess' (2007: 19) call for renewing the English classroom as a 'professional space', for both teachers and students, to engage the 'subject' of English as an 'intellectual project' that 'link[s] classroom learning to a wider theoretical enquiry', and Leung's (2005: 138) argument for the need of ELT professionals to adopt the 'ethnographic sensitivities and sensibilities' of 'epistemological relativity', 'reflexivity' and 'critical consciousness' regarding uses of language and their judgments about these in their teaching.

(7) For other discussions of such alternatives, see Canagarajah, 2006; Horner *et al.*, 2011; Lu, 2006; Matsuda and Silva, 1999.
(8) As Horner *et al.* observe, ironically, the shift in the status granted to form by this approach 'calls for *more*, not less, conscious and critical attention to how writers deploy diction, syntax, and style, as well as form, register, and media' (2011: 304).
(9) Equivalent mixtures can, of course, be found in the canonized writings affiliated with other national literatures, for example in British literature Shakespeare most obviously, but also, among countless possible examples, writings by Donne, Defoe, Swift and Woolf.
(10) Thoreau's opening to *Walden* shows him explicitly negotiating with his readers for what he appears to assume will be objections to his subject and his style.
(11) For a fuller discussion, see Lu, 1999.
(12) For discussion of a similar strategy in teaching 'French' as a language likewise 'always in translation', see Kramsch, 1998.
(13) A condensed version of parts of our argument appears in Horner (2011).

References

Arua, A. (1998) Some features of Swazi English. *World Englishes* 17 (2), 139–151.

Bamgbose, A. (1998) Torn between the norms: Innovations in world Englishes. *World Englishes* 17, 1–14.

Bartlett, L. (2009) *The Word and the World: The Cultural Politics of Literacy in Brazil*. Cresskill, NJ: Hampton Press.

Bernabé, J., Chamoiseau, P. and Confiant, R. (1989) *Éloge de la créolité*. Paris: Gallimard.

Bizzell, P. (1991) Power, authority, and critical pedagogy. *Journal of Basic Writing* 10 (2), 54–70.

Bourdieu, P. (1991) *Language and Symbolic Power* (J.B. Thompson, (ed.), G. Raymond and M. Adamson, trans.). Cambridge, MA: Harvard University Press (original work published 1982).

Burbules, N. (1986) A theory of power in education. *Educational Theory* 36, 95–114.

Burgess, T. (2007) The picture of development in Vygotskyan theory: Renewing the intellectual project of English. In V. Ellis, C. Fox and B. Street (eds) *Rethinking English in Schools: Towards a New and Constructive Stage* (pp. 19–31). London: Continuum.

Canagarajah, A. (2006) Toward a writing pedagogy of shuttling between languages: Learning from multilingual writers. *College English* 68, 589–603.

Canagarajah, A. (2007) Lingua franca English, multilingual communities, and language acquisition. *Modern Language Journal* 91, 923–939.

Coupland, N. (2000) Sociolinguistic prevarication about 'Standard English'. *Journal of Sociolinguistics* 4, 622–634.

Delbridge, A. (1999) Standard Australian English. *World Englishes* 18 (2), 259–270.

Dubin, F. (1989) Situating literacy within traditions of communicative competence. *Applied Linguistics* 10, 171–181.

Fairclough, N. (1992) The appropriacy of appropriateness. In N. Fairclough (ed.) *Critical Language Awareness* (pp. 31–56). London: Longman.

Freire, P. (1970) *Pedagogy of the Oppressed* (M. Ramos, trans.). New York: Continuum.

Friedrich, P. and Matsuda, A. (2010) When five words are not enough: A conceptual and terminological discussion of English as a lingua franca. *International Multilingual Research Journal* 4, 20–30.

Gal, S. and Irvine, J.T. (1995) The boundaries of languages and disciplines: How ideologies construct difference. *Social Research* 62, 967–1001.

Gore, J. (1992) What we can do for you! What *can* 'we' do for 'you'?: Struggling over empowerment in critical and feminist pedagogy. In C. Luke and J. Gore (eds) *Feminisms and Critical Pedagogy* (pp. 54–73). New York: Routledge.

Hay, J., MacLagan, M. and Gordon, E. (2008) *New Zealand English.* Edinburgh: Edinburgh University Press.

Horner, B. (2001) 'Students' right', English only, and re-imagining the politics of language. *College English* 63, 741–758.

Horner, B. (2011) Writing English as a lingua franca. In A. Archibald, A. Cogo and J. Jenkins (eds) *Latest Trends in ELF Research* (pp. 299–311). Cambridge: Cambridge Scholars Press.

Horner, B. and Trimbur, J. (2002) English only and US college composition. *College Composition and Communication* 53, 594–630.

Horner, B., Lu, M., Royster, J. and Trimbur, J. (2011) Language difference in writing: Toward a translingual approach. *College English* 73, 303–21.

House, J. (2003) English as a lingua franca: A threat to multilingualism? *Journal of Sociolinguistics* 7, 556–578.

Hu, X. (2004) Why China English should stand alongside British, American, and other 'World Englishes'. *English Today* 20, 26–33.

Jenkins, J. (2002) A sociolinguistically based, empirically researched pronunciation syllabus for English as an international language. *Applied Linguistics* 23 (1), 83–103.

Jenkins, J. (2006) Current perspectives on teaching world Englishes and English as a lingua franca. *TESOL Quarterly* 40 (1), 157–181.

Kirkpatrick, A. (2007) *World Englishes: Implications for International Communication and English Language Teaching.* Cambridge: Cambridge University Press.

Kirkpatrick, A. and Zhichang, X. (2002) Chinese pragmatic norms and 'China English'. *World Englishes* 21 (2), 269–272.

Kramsch, C. (1998) The privilege of the intercultural speaker. In M. Byram and M. Fleming (eds) *Language Learning in Intercultural Perspective: Approaches Through Drama and Ethnography* (pp. 16–31). Cambridge: Cambridge University Press.

Kramsch, C. (2006) The traffic in meaning. *Asia Pacific Journal of Education* 26 (1), 99–104.

Kubota, R. (2001) Teaching world Englishes to native-speakers of English in the US. *World Englishes* 20 (1), 47–64.

Lea, M. and Street, B. (1998) Student writing in higher education: An academic literacies approach. *Studies in Higher Education* 23, 157–169.

Lea, M. and Street, B. (2006) The 'academic literacies' model: Theory and applications. *Theory Into Practice* 45 (4), 368–377.

Leung, C. (2005) Convivial communication: Recontextualizing communicative competence. *International Journal of Applied Linguistics* 15, 119–144.

Lillis, T. and Scott, M. (2007) Defining academic literacies research: Issues of epistemology, ideology and strategy. *Journal of Applied Linguistics* 4, 5–32.

Lu, M. (1999) Professing multiculturalism: Teaching the politics of style. In B. Horner and M. Lu (eds) *Representing the 'Other': Basic Writers and the Teaching of Basic Writing* (pp. 166–190). Urbana, IL: National Council of Teachers of English.

Lu, M. (2004) An essay on the work of composition: Composing English against the order of fast capitalism. *College Composition and Communication* 56 (1), 16–50.

Lu, M. (2006) Living-English work. *College English* 68, 605–618.

Lu, M. and Horner, B. (1998) The problematic of experience: Redefining critical work in ethnography and pedagogy. *College English* 60, 257–277.

Luke, A. (1998) Genres of power? Literacy education and the production of capital. In R. Hasan and G. Williams (eds) *Literacy in Society* (pp. 308–338). New York: Longman.

Luke, C. (1996) Feminist pedagogy theory: Reflections on power and authority. *Educational Theory* 46, 283–302.

Matsuda, P. (2006) The myth of linguistic homogeneity in US college composition. *College English* 68 (6), 637–651.

Matsuda, P. and Silva, T. (1999) Cross-cultural composition: Mediated integration of US and international students. *Composition Studies* 27 (1), 15–30.

Mauranen, A. (2003) The corpus of English as lingua franca in academic settings. *TESOL Quarterly* 37 (3), 513–527.

'May I take your order?' (2006) – Online document. http://www.rahoi.com/2006/03/may-i-take-your-order/. Accessed 20 June 2012.

McKay, S.L. (2003) Toward an appropriate EIL pedagogy: Re-examining common ELT assumptions. *International Journal of Applied Linguistics* 13, 1–22.

Meierkord, C. (2004) Syntactic variation in interactions across international Englishes. *English World-Wide* 25 (1), 109–132.

Miller, R. (1998) The arts of complicity: Pragmatism and the culture of schooling. *College English* 61, 10–28.

Nayar, P.B. (1997) ESL/EFL dichotomy today: Language politics or pragmatics? *TESOL Quarterly* 31 (1), 9–37.

Parakrama, A. (1995) *De-hegemonizing Language Standards: Learning from (Post)colonial Englishes about 'English'*. London: MacMillan.

Pennycook, A. (2003) Global Englishes, Rip Slyme, and performativity. *Journal of Sociolinguistics* 7, 513–533.

Pennycook, A. (2008) English as a language always in translation. *European Journal of English Studies* 12 (1), 33–47.

Pennycook, A. (2010) *Language as a Local Practice*. London: Routledge.

Petraglia, J. (ed.) (1995) *Reconceiving Writing, Rethinking Writing Instruction*. Mahwah, NJ: Erlbaum.

Rubdy, R. and Saraceni, M. (2006) Introduction. In R. Rubdy and M. Saraceni (eds) *English in the World: Global Rules, Global Roles* (pp. 5–16). London: Continuum.

Seidlhofer, B. (2004) Research perspectives on teaching English as a lingua franca. *Annual Review of Applied Linguistics* 24, 209–239.

Seidlhofer, B. (2006) English as a lingua franca in the expanding circle: What it isn't. In R. Rubdy and M. Saraceni (eds) *English in the World: Global Rules, Global Roles* (pp. 40–50). London: Continuum.

Shim, R. (1999) Codified Korean English: Process, characteristics and consequence. *World Englishes* 18 (2), 247–258.

Shuck, G. (2006) Combating monolingualism: A novice administrator's challenge. *Writing Program Administration* 30 (1–2), 59–82.

Sifakis, N. (2006) Teaching EIL – teaching *international* or *intercultural* English? What teachers should know. In R. Rubdy and M. Saraceni (eds) *English in the World: Global Rules, Global Roles* (pp. 151–168). London: Continuum.

Street, B. (1984) *Literacy in Theory and Practice*. London: Cambridge University Press.

Thoreau, H.D. (1995) *Walden; Or, Life in the Woods*. New York: Dover [Boston: Ticknor] (original work published 1854).

Widdowson, H. (1994) The ownership of English. *TESOL Quarterly* 28 (2), 377–389.

Williams, R. (1977) *Marxism and Literature*. New York: Oxford University Press.

5 Multilingual and Multimodal Resources in Genre-based Pedagogical Approaches to L2 English Content Classrooms

Angel Lin

The Global Spread of English and the Desire for English-medium Education in the 'Outer and Expanding Circles'

English has become an everyday presence in many cosmopolitan cities today in both the 'outer circle' and 'expanding circle' of World Englishes (Kachru *et al.*, 2006). In international airports in Hong Kong, Seoul, Bangkok, Lima or Rio de Janeiro, bilingual or multilingual signs are everywhere, and among them there are always English signs. The global spread of English has arisen from a host of historical, political and socio-economic factors. In many 'outer circle' contexts such as Singapore, Hong Kong and Malaysia, where English was historically a colonial language imposed by former British colonial governments, English has carried with it the baggage of colonial histories and exploitations. However, today English has also become a predominant medium of global trade, science, technology, social media and the internet. For instance, it serves as a chief medium of communication for different peoples coming from both within and beyond Asia and it is a common scene in Southeast Asian cities that people of diverse ethnic backgrounds are communicating in some variety of English (see Dewey, Chapter 7, this volume).

Southeast Asia, in particular, consists of a vast array of different societies which seem to be at different historical and economic conjunctures of their respective negotiation with different kinds of modernities. However, in all their encounters with 'the West', now dispersed around the globe in various forms of globalization and global capitalism, English has become an indispensable linguistic resource they seek for themselves (though English has, in many formerly British colonies, been present to varying extents in the administration and education structures for a long time). The governments in these countries, in their respective socio-ecnomic contexts, are often infused with a desire for development, modernity and human resource capital for successful participation in the new global economic order. Such capital includes English with respect to information/communication technology, business management and commercial know-how and so on, and very often English comes in a package with all these desirable 'goodies', or is considered the indispensable medium for bringing in and acquiring these goodies. How to enable students to cross the English divide, how to make English linguistic capital (and which English varieties) accessible to more of the school population and how to spread English capital more efficiently and evenly across different social sectors in the society, have become important issues in language policy and English across the curriculum pedagogical research. These concerns very often occupy priority places in national development agendas. For instance, in many Southeast Asian societies today, serious government attention is given to the notion of using English-medium education programmes to promote the use and learning of English. Below I shall illustrate with the case of Hong Kong some of the dilemmas and difficulties associated with English-medium education in these contexts and how a proposal of introducing multilingualism, multimodalities and genre-based pedagogies into the L2 English content classroom might offer a way out of these dilemmas.

The Policy Context of L2 English-medium Education in Hong Kong

The current policy dilemma in Hong Kong is how to ensure that students' proficiency in English can be improved, while avoiding the social and educational costs of the previous policy of linguistic streaming (in 1998 schools were streamed into English-medium or Chinese-medium and since then the Chinese-medium schools have been labelled by society as second-rate; see review of this policy in Lin & Man, 2009). Parental demand for access to English-medium schools is extremely strong and the imposition of restrictions of access through streaming is perceived as inequitable and as reproductive of the structures of privilege that existed in colonial times. Twelve years after the introduction of the 1998 streaming policy, the government is relaxing or destabilizing the strict boundary between the Chinese-medium Instruction (CMI) schools and English-medium instruction (EMI) schools. Starting from September 2010, over 300 former CMI secondary schools in Hong Kong are allowed to switch the medium of instruction (MOI) to English for some of their academic subjects or for some percentage of the lesson time of each of their academic subjects under the new 'fine-tuning MOI policy' of the Hong Kong Education Bureau. Many CMI schools have chosen to change the MOI of one or two of their academic subjects (usually Science or Mathematics, but in some schools Geography or Economics too) or some percentage of the lessons of each of their academic subjects from CMI to EMI. One pressing question, however, remains: what kind of bridging curriculum and pedagogy will help (former CMI) basic English proficiency students to cope with changing their learning medium to English?

The Need for Innovative Approaches to L2 English Content Instruction

In view of the above difficulties and dilemmas, there is the need to break away from rigid linguistic streaming models to develop fexible, productive pedagogies for L2 English content classrooms, as other authors in this volume have outlined. Once educators and policy-makers can think outside of the box and break away from the static concept of languages as discrete monolithic entities then they might find a whole new space for exploration of innovative means to achieve reachable goals in both English learning and content learning. I shall turn to a discussion of four directions that might offer potential for developing innovative ways out of our difficulties and dilemmas: (i) developing multiple flexible approaches to content-based L2 instruction; (ii) breaking away from the traditional immersion model as the only best approach to designing L2 English content programmes; (iii) drawing on multimodal and continua theories of langauge and communication; and (iv) drawing on genre-based multilingual, multimodal and popular cultural resources to provide basic-L2-proficiency students with access to L2 academic content and literacy.

(i) Developing multiple flexible approaches to content-based L2 English instruction

In traditional thinking about approaches to designing bilingual education, there is a sharp boundary drawn between teaching L2 English as a subject and using L2 English as the MOI for teaching content. However, in exploring innovative approaches to designing L2 English content pro-grammes, such a rigid boundary needs to be crossed over or destabilized. Figure 5.1 shows a new way of thinking: teaching L2 English as a subject and using L2 English as an MOI for teaching content does not need to be seen as two discrete programme models but as lying on two end-points of a con-tinuum on the horizontal-axis in Figure 5.1. If educators could expand their thinking in this direction, they would be able to design multiple flexible approaches to L2 English content programmes. For instance, in many Southeast Asian contexts where L2 English teaching resources do not exist in abundance (e.g. not enough English fluent teachers to use L2 English as the sole MOI for teaching content subjects), a strong content-based L2 English programme can be developed, which can serve as a good-enough programme with the existing resources to make L2 English academic litera-cies accessible to the majority of students (e.g. English academic registers and genres, lexicogrammatical knowledge and skills relevent to these genres). Side by side with content subjects taught in L1 (i.e. first language, which ensures that the content teaching goals are reached), there can be a content-based English L2 curriculum taught as an accompanying English academic literacy enrichment programme. I propose one step further, that if in some 'outer or expanding circle' contexts where the implementation of L2 English as an MOI for any content subjects is not feasible given inadequate teaching resources (e.g. EMI staff members), then the development of a strong L2

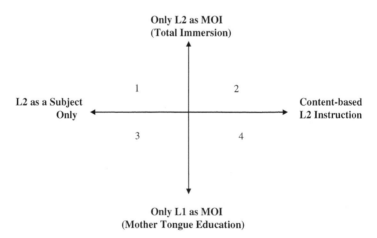

Figure 5.1 Crisscrossing spectrums of content-based L2 instruction and L2 immersion for designing innovative approaches to bilingual education

English enrichment programme that has a focus on the academic registers of some key content subjects (see also a review of different English as a Second Language (ESL) programmes in the mainstream programme options in Davison & Williams, 2001) is a good choice as a possible mode of providing some access to English academic registers (see also review of programme options in Lin & Man, 2009).

In Thailand, for instance, the Sarasas Ektra Bilingual School has pioneered an 'immerse twice' model (Jones, 2007), which consists of a two-track curriculum: key content areas are taught in the students' L1 in one track, and the same key content areas (with a less packed but equally challenging content syllabus that is covering less content information but retaining the discipline-specific methods of inquiry) are taught in English (L2 of the students) in the parallel track to the same students. In fact the English instruction on content matter can be seen as a content-based English for Academic Purposes (EAP) instruction, and not as an 'immersion programme' in the sense described in the traditional bilingual education literature. In many Southeast Asian states, where content curriculums tend to be packed with information items to prepare students for public examinations on these subjects, this two-track system enables students to cover all the curriculum content for public examinations in the L1, while at the same time allowing for ample exposure of the students to learning the discipline-specific academic registers in the L2. This two-track system seems to be workable in this context of the Sarasas Bilingual School, where the majority of students are expecting to continue their studies in local Thai universities that, however, offer some programmes in English (e.g. international business studies). I have observed classes and interviewed students in this school and found that the students were not bored by having to learn the subjects 'twice', as the subject curriculums, in the words of the students, 'are organized differently and taught by different teachers'. The students feel that this approach has both reinforced their understanding of the content subjects and increased their English ability to learn these content subjects. The students' public examination scores also show high levels of both academic attainment and English language attainment. While this approach might need to be adapted for it to be workable in other contexts, it does provide an innovative way of thinking when one explores new solutions for old dilemmas.

(ii) Breaking away from the 'immersion' thinking

Another innovative way of thinking about flexible approaches to L2 English content instruction might involve the need to break away from the immersion model as the best approach to EMI education. As an increasing number of studies on the potential positive benefits of making use of L1 resources (e.g. Lin, 2006) have shown, strategically and systematically using L1 can help to bridge the gap between the students' existing L2 proficiency and the required L2 proficiency to learn in the L2. This proposal will be explored further in the sections below.

(iii) Multimodal and continua theories of language and communication

As mentioned above, one of the pedagogical straitjackets imposed by much official and public discourse in Southeast Asian contexts is that of 'bilingualism through monolingualism': that is, to use only the target language as the medium of instruction in the classroom with the hope that students will become bilingual through such monolingual total immersion classes, denigrating and excluding the L1 resources of the students from the L2 classroom. Fuelled by the native-speaker myth (i.e. only teachers speaking the students' L2 as their 'mother tongue' should ideally be employed as teachers in L2 classrooms), the more monolingual the teachers are, the more 'pure' and valued they seem to be in many Southeast Asian contexts because then they are believed to be using only the L2 of the students without any code-switching or mixing. This is an entrenched theme in official policy discourse that has been critiqued by researchers (Lin, 2000a; Luk & Lin, 2005).

Much of such public and official discourse has derived its legitimacy and authority from some version of Second Language Acquisition (SLA) theory that has not been informed by more recent developments in multimodal and continua theories of language and communication. Language (e.g. L1, L2, L3) should not be seen and planned as discrete separate entities but rather as continua (Hornberger, 2003; Canagarajah, 2005) and language communication can only be fully understood if it is analyzed as part of multimodal communication (Kress & van Leeuwen, 1996, 2001). Recent critical sociolinguists also argue that language as a local practice is inherently plural and multiple and it has been the categorizing ideologies of colonialism and modern state nationalism that have imposed boundaries and categories on language (Pennycook, 2003, 2010).

Multimodality analysis as applied to the analysis of the curriculum practices of science teaching and learning (Kress *et al.*, 2001) is especially useful for our purposes here. The multimodal analytical tools used to analyze textbook visuals and graphics are useful in enhancing teachers' and students' awareness of how textbooks and curriculum practices (including teachers' gestures, demonstrations, actions and blackboard drawings) present and construct certain views of the nature and status of science knowledge which are by no means natural, neutral or universal but reflecting certain ideological stances. By introducing teachers and students to some of these multimodal analytical tools, teachers' and students' communicative repertoire of multimodal resources useful for teaching and learning content subjects will also be enhanced.

(iv) Drawing on genre-based multilingual and multimodal resources to provide basic-L2-proficiency students with access to L2 academic content and literacy

Lin's (2006) study shows how a bilingual science teacher uses a bilingual teaching approach to provide basic-English-proficiency students with access to the English science discourse. While critics may say that students will be deprived of the much-needed L2 exposure to learn how to give explanations, arguments and examples in L2, one has to acknowledge that what the teacher is doing is basically helping students to understand the L2 science discourse in the L2 curriculum and texts and to be able to respond with appropriate L2 science discourse to questions in the L2 science curriculum. Lemke, in his book on science classrooms (1990), concludes that learning science basically involves the learning or acquiring of a set of science discourses and their relations. For instance, mastering the science concept of 'photosynthesis' means, among other things, being able to produce in speech and writing a science definition of the concept (e.g. 'Photosynthesis is the process by which solar energy is converted into food energy by green plants'). Mastering science is thus mastering the discourses, rhetorics (Kress *et al.*, 2001) or discipine-specific ways of expressing/constructing scientific concepts and theories and the interrelationships among them. The bilingual teacher seems to be providing a rich L1 semantic context of L1 lifeworld examples and experiences familiar to the students to embed the presentation of the lexicogrammatical elements of the L2 science discourse to facilitate students' understanding of L2 science discourses (i.e. the concepts and theories mediated in specific L2 science lexicogrammatical expressions such as 'matter is made up of small particles', 'particles are in continuous motion', 'this is called Kinetic Theory'). It is important to notice that the mastering of the science discourses (or the science genres) is not automatic and involves a lot of concrete illustrations of these abstract general concepts with familiar daily life examples, and the corresponding shuttling to and fro between the L2 science discourses and the familiar L1 lifeworld discourses (Luke *et al.* 2004). Given this situation, it is difficult for basic-English-proficiency students to access (e.g. understand and acquire) the English science discourse without the linguistic and cultural bridging functions offered by the

L1 semantic context that the bilingual teacher provides as well as the multiple modes of science teaching, espeically visual modes (Kress *et al.*, 2001). While the students might not have exposure to English for giving lively explanations and examples, the students are at least helped to access and acquire the English science discourse through the use of bilingual/multilingual and multimodal resources.

However, if the above sounds too much like the 'Identify and Induct' paradigm of recent studies in academic literacies (see critique of the 'Identify and Induct' approach by Street, 2004; Lea & Street, 1998; and Lillis & Scott, 2007, from an 'academic literacies' perspective), it has to be pointed out that the genre-based approach can be coupled with a critical awareness raising. While students are being apprenticed into science discourse genres, teachers can also simultaneously draw students' attention to the social-historical constructedness of these genres (or discipline-specific ways of expressing/seeing/ viewing the world) and thus the potential for students' own transformation of the genres in their own works. As Kress and van Leeuwen (1996) point out:

> Teaching the rules of writing has not meant the end of creative uses of language in literature and elsewhere, and teaching visual skills will not spell the end of the arts. (Kress & van Leeuwen, 1996: 3)

Likewise, teaching the genres and rhetorics of science discourse does not necessarily turn students into blind followers of these genres and rhetorics if the teaching is done in a way to stress the constructedness (and deconstructing the universalness) of science knowledge.

The key point here is that genre theory is used not only to describe what students read and write but to *design* how they are taught. This involves a pedagogy that asks:

> How can we develop teachers who are authorities, without being authoritarian? How can we develop students who control the distinctive discourses of their culture, and at the same time are not simply co-opted by them but approach them critically with a view to renovation – to challenging the social order which the discourses they are learning sustain? (Martin, 2010: Slide 81)

To summarize this section on innovative approaches to L2 English content instruction, if we revisit Figure 5.1 and utilize the criss-crossing of the horizontal axis and the vertical axis to design innovative approaches to the design and provision of bilingual education, we can put different innovative combinations of approaches in the different quadrants. For instance, in quadrant two, we can have both L1 as MOI for certain content subjects and an additional component of content-based L2 instruction (e.g. the option being implemented in Malaysia now). In quadrant four, we can have only L2 content-based L2 instruction (as the 'shoe-string budget' bilingual education mentioned above). In addition, we can combine quadrants, such as quadrants 2 and 4, as in the Sarasas Ektra Bilingual School in Thailand discussed above. Different innovative approaches to language policy and planning (LPP) can be explored to suit the local needs and availability of resources in different contexts once educators and policy-makers can break away from traditional immersion approaches to the provision of bilingual education.

In the above sections I have focused on the importance of breaking away from traditional discrete language and immersion models of thinking about L2 content classrooms.

In the following sections I shall outline the theoretical framework of a genre-based bridging pedagogy that draws on multilingualism and multimodalities to help basic-English-proficiency students to develop L2 English academic literacy. This emphasis in the second half of this discussion aims to illustrate with some concrete pedagogical examples how breaking away from monolingual immersion and discrete language models can create a new space for exploring innovative, multilingual and multimodal strategies in L2 content classrooms.

Proposing a Genre-based, Multilingual and Multimodal Bridging Pedagogy

This section outlines the theoretical framework of a bridging pedagogy that I am currently developing in the Hong Kong junior secondary school context. I draw on multiple theoretical traditions in applied/educational linguistics and propose a genre-based, multilingual, multimodal framework for developing a bridging curriculum for Hong Kong secondary schools to assist students in making the transition from CMI to L2 English academic learning. The theoretical frameworks drawn upon are: (1) Halliday's linguistic theory of 'grammatical metaphor' – its pivotal role in the abstraction and technicalization of the language of science as well as Kress and van Leeuvan's Halliday-informed and inspired multimodality analysis; (2) the Sydney School of genre analysis and genre-based pedagogy for academic literacy development; and (3) bilingual education and ESL theories of bridging pedagogies. Central to the proposed framework are the principles of genre-based pedagogy (Martin & Rose, 2008; Rose, 2008) and Gibbons' (2009) methods of 'designed scaffolding and bridging'. While Gibbons' methods can be seen as lying on the level of classroom techniques, the principle underlying her methods is that of using multiple resources (including students' familiar linguistic resources such as their L1) to assist students in accessing the curriculum. This principle is in line with our overall theoretical framework of drawing on multiple linguistic and multimodal resources in curriculum design and practices.

Multiple Theoretical Traditions

In the following sections the useful theoretical traditions will be outlined. Due to limited space these are not meant to be comprehensive delineations of the theories but just synoptic outlines to bear on the present discussion on how to assist students in participating in L2 English content lessons.

(1) Development of knowledge and the language of science: The linguistic and multimodal processes of 'packing' and 'unpacking' English science texts

Halliday (1998) views language development as the development of a child's potential for creating meaning (or the child's 'semogenic' capacity). This semogenic development is conceived as a growing linguistic ability to transform *experience* into language-based *meaning*. Knowledge development is thus closely linked to linguistic development under Halliday's model of language and knowledge: as a child moves from common sense knowledge to educational knowledge and to technical knowledge, the child has to be assisted in learning to move in and out of the different linguistic processes of 'packing' and 'unpacking' the language of science or the language of abstraction and technicality. 'School knowledge is prototypically made of language' (Halliday, 1998: 25), and acquiring the knowledge of science entails acquiring the specific linguistic and multimodal ways of making meaning (e.g. of speaking and writing, of action sequence in conducting experiments) in the science disciplines/communities. These specific linguistic ways of making meaning cannot be expected to be naturally picked up by a child and need to be explicitly taught to the novice.

The main characteristic of the language of science and the main barrier to the learner in tackling science texts is related to the use of 'grammatical metaphor' in educational and technical language. Grammatical metaphor, as articulated by Halliday (1993, 1998, 2004), refers to the specific linguistic processes of 'packing' dynamic, concrete action processes (realized linguistically as verbal clauses) into static, abstract entities and their (logical) relations (realized linguistically as nominal groups); for instance, the everyday oral language of sentence (i) (in a linear, temporal, storytelling/narrative mode) is 'packed' into the technical language of sentence (ii) (in a 'Y is caused by X', non-linear, explanatory logic) below:

(i)   The driver drove the bus too fast down the hill, so the brakes failed.

(ii) The brake failure was caused by the driver's overrapid driving of the bus downhill.

Thus a Secondary 2 (Grade 8) student is likely to encounter school texts with sentences like the following one:

(iii) Waste gases released by motor vehicles, power stations and factories are the main sources of air pollution in Hong Kong. (From a Secondary 2 Integrated Science textbook commonly used in EMI schools.)

To 'unpack' academic language for students, a competent EMI teacher might typically transform (or translate) sentence (iii) into everyday language that usually consists of the following assemble of sentences delivered in an IRF (Initiation-Response-Feedback) classroom discourse format (Sinclair & Coulthard, 1975; Heap, 1985; Lin, 2007); such IRF exchanges function to engage students in talking about the text, to relate the textbook topic to students' daily life experience, and to get students interested:

T:	Why do we have air pollution in Hong Kong? What are the things that pollute the air? What are the things that make the air dirty, making it smelly or bad for people? Can you give me some examples? What are the things that make the air bad and the bad air will make you sick?
S1/S2/S3:	Factories! Cars! Smoking!
T:	Yes, very good! Cars, factories, what else? What other things can you think of?
S4:	Power companies!
T:	Yes, very good! Power companies, power stations ... So, let's look at the textbook, page 65, first paragraph, it says: *Waste gases released by motor vehicles, power stations and factories are the main sources of air pollution in Hong Kong.* So, now, you

know the main sources of air pollution in Hong Kong, do you‹ The cars, the power stations and factories, they give out waste gases, dirty gases, and so these dirty gases pollute our air and make people sick, right‹

The above reconstructed classroom exchanges (based on many years of classroom observation in Hong Kong schools) is readily recognizable by teachers as a common pedagogic strategy in rendering the school academic texts accessible and interesting to students. It illustrates how teachers are engaged in the linguistic/interactive processes of 'unpacking' academic texts for students in their daily teaching. When the students' English proficiency is limited and even English paraphrasing (as shown above) might not help the unpacking of academic texts, the teacher might draw on L1 resources to assist with the unpacking process as shown in the reconstructed dialogue below (English translations of the Cantonese utterances are placed in angle brackets immediately after the utterances):

T: Why do we have air pollution in Hong Kong‹
S: [no response]
T: [slowly] So, why do we have air pollution in Hong Kong‹ What are the things that pollute the air‹
S: [no response]
T: Air pollution，咩係 <what is> air pollution 呀 <question particle>‹
S: 空氣 <air>…
T: 空氣咩呢 <air what>‹
S: 空氣污染 <air pollution>!
T: Yes，空氣污染 <air pollution>，即係 <that is> air pollution。咁點解會有 <so why is there> air pollution 呢 <question particle>‹ 咩野會做成 <what will lead to> air pollution 呢 <question particle>‹ 個 <the> source 係咩呢 <is what>‹
S: 汽車D廢氣 <cars' waste gas>!
T: 係喇 <yes>，汽車D廢氣係其中一個源頭 <cars' waste gas is one of the sources>，其中一個 <one of the> source。仲有D咩 <what are the other> source 呢 <question particle>‹
S: 工廠D廢氣…車D廢氣…食煙… <factories' waste gas… cars' waste gas… smoking…>
T: 工廠D廢氣點用英文講 <factories' waste gas, how to say it in English>‹ 工廠係 <factory is>…
S: Factory!
T: 係喇 <yes>, factory。咁廢氣呢 <then how about waste gas>‹
S: air…

T: no, not air. 廢氣唔係叫做 <waste gas is not called> air，係 <it's> waste gases。Waste gases，即係廢氣 <that is waste gases>。

S: 哦 (Yes) ...

T: 哦 (Yes)，咁即係咩呢 <so, what does that mean>? 除咗 <apart from> waste gases，仲有咩野其他源頭呀 <what are the other sources>?

S: 空氣污染嘅源頭有汽車D廢氣、工廠D廢氣同食煙D廢氣 <The sources of air pollution are car waste gas, factory waste gas and smoking's waste gas>。

T: Right. Any other sources? ... No? no other sources? 無其他源頭噃 <No other sources>? OK, so, let's look at the textbook, page 65, first paragraph, it says: *Waste gases released by motor vehicles, power stations and factories are the main sources of air pollution in Hong Kong.* 噃，睇吓呢句 <Okay, look at this sentence> *Waste gases released by motor vehicles, power stations and factories* ... motor vehicles 同 <and> factories 你地都講啱咗 <you are all correct about>，但無講到 <but you haven't talked about> power stations 喎 <still>。咁咩係 <So, what are> power stations 呀 <question particle>? What is a power station?

S: 係地鐵站 <It's subway station>!

T: 唔係地鐵站 <It's not subway station>，地鐵站係 <subway station is> MTR station，你答啱一半啫 <You're only half correct>。咩係 <What is> power station 呀 <question particle>? 仲有D咩 <Are there any other> station 呀 <question particle>? 唔係車站呀吓 <Remember it's not a train station>?

S: 發電站<Power station>!

T: 係喇<Yes>，right! 係發電站 <It's power station>。Very good! Power station 就即係發電站喇 <is power station>。咁究竟咩野會做成 <So, what will lead to> air pollution 嘅 sources 呢 <air pollution's sources>? Look at the textbook again, *Waste gases released by motor vehicles, power stations and factories are the main sources of air pollution in Hong Kong.* So now you know the meaning of this sentence, right? Now you know the main sources of air pollution in Hong Kong, do you? The cars, the power stations and factories, they give out waste gases, dirty gases, and so these dirty gases pollute our air and make people sick, right? 咁呢D空氣污染嘅源頭就整到我地病喇 <So, these air pollution sources make us sick> ...

In the above reconstructed classroom exchanges, I illustrate how the teacher uses both L1 everyday language and examples and L1 formal technical language (e.g. waste gases, sources of air pollution) to unpack the L2 academic text for his students. Teachers can also enhance their ability of unpacking

Table 5.1 Using a simple table to contrast L1 and L2 resources

L2 academic language	L2 everyday language	L1/L2 code-mixing (academic language)	L1 academic language
What are the sources of air pollution	What makes the air dirty?	咩野會做成 air pollution (空氣污染) 呢?	空氣污染嘅源頭 係 咩野
Waste gases	Dirty gases	(污漕空氣, i.e., 廢氣, waste gases)	廢氣

science texts for students using visuals (Kress *et al.*, 2001) and graphic organizers (Kress & van Leeuwen, 1996). For instance, just tabulating the L1 and L2 expressions in a contrastive table will help students to grasp the L2 technical language using L1 resources (Table 5.1). Of course, other visual images regarding the sources of pollution can be used. Students can also be asked to draw multilingual comic strips in groups to brainstorm about the sources of pollution in Hong Kong and the world. Socio-linguists and new literacies researchers have, for instance, researched the rising use of multilingual resources in the new media among young people in recent years (Androutsopoulos, 2006, 2007, 2008; Lin, 2008a); drawing on new digital and popular cultural resources such as YouTube videos on science topics will also help link students' everyday popular cultural worlds with their school worlds (Lin & Man, 2011).

We can see that multiple linguistic (including L1 informal and formal lexicogrammatical resources) and multimodal resources are useful in making academic texts accessible and interesting to students and this is summarized in Figure 5.2.

While unpacking academic texts for students is very important, what is missing in many classrooms, however, is the explicit modelling and mentoring of the linguistic processes of 'packing' or 'repacking'; that is, to assist students to progressively move from everyday oral language to educational and technical language, and this has to be part of, in tandem with, an L2 academic literacy programme. It is to this second related theoretical tradition that I shall turn in the next section.

(2) Genre analysis theory and genre-based pedagogy for academic literacy development: Modelling and mentoring academic genres in the context of shared experience

What students need to learn to 'pack', 'unpack' and 'repack' in order to succeed in navigating the textual world of the school is not just condensed

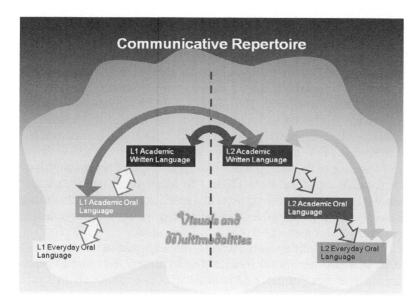

Figure 5.2 Bridging multiple resources – ultimate goal: Expanded repertoire

nominal groups (grammatical metaphors) at sentence level, but also the genres of academic texts. Discipline-specific genres consolidate the knowledge patterns of a specific discipline and both co-textualize it and contextualize it with respect to related knowledge. Genres are 'consolidation displays' or 'storage devices'/knowledge configurations that have evolved in specific communities of an academic discipline. Building on Halliday's systemic functional linguistics, the Sydney School of genre analysis further developed theoretical and analytical tools of 'discourse semantics' (i.e. analyzing meaning patterns beyond the clause level) (Martin, 1992; Martin & Rose, 2007). While there are other schools of pedagogically oriented genre analysis (e.g. the New Rhetoric group (cf. Russell *et al.*, 2009), or genre analysis in the ESP (English for Specific Purposes) traditions; cf. Prior & Hengst, 2010), the Sydney School of genre analysis has had a long tradition of developing a school-based pedagogy for working with primary and secondary students using the genre-based approach to academic literacy development (e.g. Martin & Painter, 1986; Martin, 1989, 1990; Derewianka, 1990; Rothery, 1990, 1994, 1996; Martin & Rose, 2008).

David Rose's website, *Reading to Learn*, has served as a knowledge exchange nexus to apply genre analysis theory to the everyday work of teachers, supporting a school-based pedagogy for scaffolding students' academic literacy development (http://www.readingtolearn.com.au/). The Sydney School's genre-based academic literacy pedagogy can be summarized in Rose's (2008) Reading to Learn Cycle (Figure 5.3). (In adopting this approach I also acknowledge the usefulness of other genre approaches developed in the literature which can all inform our curriculum practice; e.g. Swales, 1990, 2004; Russell *et al.*, 2009; Bhatia, 2001.) It hinges on the importance of explicit modelling and mentoring students about the features of specific academic genres through the cycle of: (i) Deconstruction (teacher models to students how to analyze genre schematic structure and sentence patterns of reading texts) (see Figure 5.4 for an example of genre analysis of an informational report on Barn Owls), (ii) Joint Construction (teacher assists students in co-constructing texts in a specific genre and joint-writing of sentences), and (iii) Independent Construction (students independently write sentences and construct texts in a specific genre).

Such explicit modelling and mentoring, however, has to take place in a context of shared experience instead of through mere lecturing of genre structure and sentence features. And to avoid an over-emphasis on linguistic

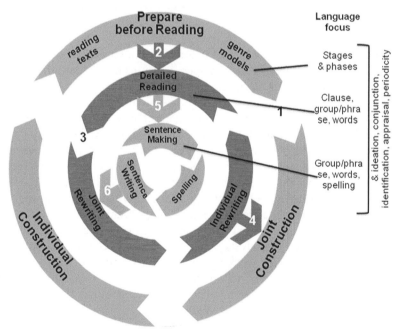

Figure 5.3 The reading to learn cycle
(*Source*: Rose, 2008)

structures, emphasis has to be given to providing a multimodal context for the curriculum topic. How to establish a rich multimodal curriculum context of meaningful experience shared by teachers and students is essential to the success of explicit modelling and mentoring of academic literacies. For instance, explicit modelling of text analysis (e.g. Figure 5.4) should come only after a meaningful context of shared experience has been established (e.g. the context of writing an informational report on the kinds of interesting living things that one can find in the campus or neighbourhood. The 'Write it Right' – Sydney Metropolitan East Disadvantaged Schools Program (Rothery, 1994), for instance, provides resources to teachers and students to carry out a genre-based pedagogy for academic literacy learning. As academic knowledge lives mainly in writing, or reading texts that also integrate visuals, images and increasingly sound too, and only a fraction of the discipline-specific knowledge can be covered orally in class, reading is crucial. Students have to learn to read academic texts. In the teacher-student joint reading and writing processes, an important unpacking and repacking context is created. Through teacher-student joint reading, students are apprenticed into using the unpacking/reading strategies to extract useful concepts and their logical relations from the text and to

---

Text type: Expository Report
- Describing things (parts of wholes: giving information on aspects or parts of one thing)
- A Report on Barn Owls (written by 2 children following joint work by their class)

Language features
- Constant use of subject reference
- Use simple present tense
- Use verbs for behavior (*eats, fly, pick up*)
- Subject and verb generally consistent with some exceptions; e.g. *The Barn Owl... they*
- Use simple sentence structures, with connectives such as *because, so that*

Purpose and organization
- Has a general classification as orientation
- Has description grouped under subheadings
- Includes physical and behavioral characteristics
- Uses subheadings to define paragraphs
- Each paragraph begins with a reference to the subejct, e.g. ˅ *The Barn owls...*, *"It...*"
- Uses explanation appropriately to conclude text

A Report on Barn Owls

The Barn Owl is a bird of prey. It is an endangered species. It lives in barns and trees. They are nocturnal.

Description
Its face is like a plate which is used as a satellite dish. The sound bounces off.

The colour
It has brown speckles and a white face.
It has white under the wings and a white belly.
There are furry-speckled feathers on its back.

Habitat
The Barn Owl lives in barns and chimneys.
The Barn Owl does not make nests.

Food
It is a carnivore and it eats mice, rats, wild gerbils and baby rabbits.

Movement/Speed
The Barn Owls fly fast and silent and glides and it flies low, so that their prey can't hear it coming. The Owl is endangered because people are moving to barns and also because mice eat chemicals and the owls eat the mice and they die.

Ways of describing
- Use adjectives and noun, e.g. *sharp claws furry speckled feathers, endangered species*
- Frequently use very specific adjectives, e.g. *satellite* dish
- Use an appropriate simile, e.g. *face like a plate*

Figure 5.4 Modeling explicit analysis of a simple science report: The Barn Owl
(*Source*: Adapted from Rees, 1996: 57)

re/present this content in visuals (e.g. graphic organizers, diagrams to enhance students' grasp of the scientific concepts and their logical relations). Through teacher-student joint writing, students are apprenticed into using the repacking/writing strategies to re-textualize the graphically represented information and logical relations into appropriate text types in the discipline. However, how can these joint-reading and joint-writing processes be enabled among EFL (English as a Foreign Language) students who might still have gaps in their English proficiency?

(3) Bilingual education theories of scaffolding and bridging in L2 academic literacy development

As the Sydney School genre-based academic literacy pedagogy has been developed mainly for scaffolding L1 students (albeit always including disadvantaged and indigenous/linguistic minority groups in their development phases), one needs to turn to bilingual education theories and L2/ESL academic literacy pedagogies for theoretical and pedagogical input on how best to bridge the L2 academic literacy development of L2 learners (e.g. English as an L2 might be a language used only in the school context and not in the everyday life of the students and their families and in the wider society – as in Hong Kong, China or many East Asian societies).

Such an L2 context often means that multiple gaps exist not only in the students' L2 academic literacy knowledge and skills, but also in their L2 oral everyday language and oral academic language skills, as well as L1 oral and written academic language skills (see Figure 5.2). How to scaffold students in such a context so that they can acquire L2 academic literacy presents a daunting task to educational linguists, researchers and teachers. Apart from drawing on the Sydney approach to genre-based pedagogy, teachers can also draw on other useful genre-based pedagogical approaches (e.g. Swales, 1990; Bhatia, 2001; Paltridge, 2009, 2011) in developing their own situated approaches fit for their own purposes.

Cummins' L1-L2 interdependence theory and notions of BICS (Basic Interpersonal Communication Skills) and CALP (Cognitive Academic Language Proficiency) in bilingual education (Cummins, 1991) have informed us on the important role that L1 language and literacy can play in the learning of L2 language and literacy (see review of Cummins' theories in Lin & Man, 2009). In particular, it has informed Gibbons' (2009) pedagogy of scaffolding and bridging ESL students' academic literacy development through *rich tasks* and *high support – that is, learning in the challenge zone*. Gibbons' (2009) observation that many ESL literacy curriculums have been characterized by low-level mechanical drills and intellectually unchallenging tasks is also very true of the situation in many Hong Kong schools (Lin, 1999, 2000b). A preliminary analysis of the Integrated Science English textbooks commonly used in Band 2–3 schools in Hong Kong (Lin & Wong, 2011) shows that the textbook language is truncated and made up of almost point-form text and provides little modelling of coherent text types found in the science discipline (e.g. informational reports, explanatory texts). Students are provided with mainly simplified English language in these textbooks (i.e. serving the 'unpacking function', but there is little exposure to well-written academic text types; i.e. no support for 'repacking').

In light of the current Hong Kong situation, I find Gibbons' works (1993, 2002, 2008, 2009) especially instructive. Below I summarize the principles from Gibbons (2009: 154–158) on how to do designed scaffolding and bridging in content-based ESL programmes:

(1) Programmes build on students' prior knowledge and their current language skills (both their mother tongue and their second language), while at the same time embracing new content and language goals.
(2) Clear and explicit programme goals are shared with the students.
(3) Tasks are sequenced so that each task serves as the 'building block' for the subsequent task.
(4) A variety of organizational structures is used (pair work, group work, individual work, teacher-directed whole-class work).
(5) The curriculum is *amplified*, not simplified: teachers use 'message abundancy' (i.e. key ideas are presented in many different ways, including rhetoric strategies and genres, visuals and images, as well as academic social practices such as classroom/laboratory inquiry practices).

While these principles have been tried out and proved useful in ESL contexts in Australia, they remain untested in L2 contexts where English is used mainly in the school and not in the everyday life of the students (e.g. English in Hong Kong; see Li, 2009; Lin, 1999, 2008b). In the Hong Kong policy context, research in this area has been made difficult during the past decade given the government's linguistic streaming policy implemented in 1998, which maintained a strict division of 'pure English' or 'pure mother tongue' in segregating schools into EMI and CMI schools. The 2010 implementation of the fine-tuning MOI policy in Hong Kong witnesses a relaxation of MOI policy options and new options are now open to CMI schools, which can opt for using English in some of their content subjects or in some portions of a selected content subject. Exactly how this is to be done in terms of classroom language practices is largely left to the devices of the schools, which often try out different methods randomly. It is out of this urgent need of many Hong Kong schools for theoretically based and empirically grounded principles for guiding their pedagogy that the present pedagogical model is proposed.

Proposing a Genre-based Multilingual and Multimodal Bridging Pedagogy for the Integrated Science Subject in Hong Kong Junior Secondary Schools

In this section I propose a multilingual and multimodal pedagogy for the Integrated Science subject in junior secondary schools in Hong Kong, as a pilot model for future research in this area for other L2 English content subjects in other L2 contexts. The model draws on genre-based pedagogical principles developed by Martin and Rose (2008) and Rose (2008), the bridging pedagogical principles proposed by Gibbons (2009) (see above) as well as the findings of science educators of EFL and ESL students (Fang, 2006; Janzen, 2008) and these principles are summarized below:

- Explicit modelling and mentoring of academic genre schematic structure and language patterns and features in a rich meaningful curriculum context of shared experience that is supported by rich visuals and multimodalities, including the use of images, graphic organizers, diagrams and (YouTube) videos on science experiments and activities: for example, how to make a tornado in a bottle; this YouTube video can provide a rich experiential context for stimulating students to think, talk, discuss, read and write explanatory texts in joint-activities with the teacher: http://www.youtube.com/watch?v=reEQfFVeJUw.
- Explicit joint-analysis with students of the lexical and grammatical features of science or academic language including analysis of complex nominal groups and science/academic word-formation processes (Fang, 2006).
- It is informed by Gibbons' (2009) principles of ESL bridging pedagogy (see above); in particular, the curriculum is *amplified*, not simplified: teachers use 'message abundancy' (i.e. key ideas are presented in many different ways, including visuals, multimodalities and multiple linguistic resources).
- It is informed by science educators' pedagogical principles: diverse instructional strategies including group work, hands-on activities and multiple forms of input are used (Janzen, 2008).

- Science classroom interactions are linked to an academic literacy (reading and writing) programme that comprises teacher-student joint reading and joint writing leading gradually to student independent reading and writing (see Figure 5.3).
- Through professional development collaboration the teacher and researcher engage in co-lesson planning and co-teaching, with the aim of enhancing expertise in both teacher and researcher (with the teacher acquiring academic literacy mentoring skills, and the researcher acquiring expertise in interweaving academic literacy teaching into the science curriculum) (e.g. see the integrated approaches to academic literacies of Mitchell, 2006).
- Before entering into the above professional development stage, naturalistic classroom observations are conducted to enable the research team to design the pedagogic intervention strategies that are suited to the contextual and curriculum needs of the class (see studies in this area; e.g. Hornberger & McKay, 2010; Paltridge, 2009, 2011; Kress *et al.*, 2001).
- During the post-professional development period, no co-lesson planning/co-teaching takes place and naturalistic classroom observations are conducted to see if there is sustained effect of the earlier pedagogical support.

Coda

Future research is needed to both explore and test out the effectiveness of different innovative multilingual and multimodal approaches to the provision of English academic literacy in the 'expanding circle' contexts as these contexts are increasingly infused with the desire to acquire the necessary English (L2) academic skills to participate in the global knowledge economy. Such desires are not fantasies if we can break away from traditional models of monolingual immersion education which have emerged from contexts radically different from those of many Southeast Asian societies. Languages (e.g. L1, L2, L3) should not be seen and planned as discrete separate entities but rather as continua (Hornberger, 2003; Canagarajah, 2005). Likewise, L2 English content education programmes can also be designed and developed not as discrete models but as lying on criss-crossing continua (e.g. Figure 5.1). With such flexible non-categorical thinking we can perhaps alleviate much of the undesirable labelling effect associated with streaming students categorically into different discrete L1 and L2 immersion programmes. There is thus a strong need, in our own respective contexts, to do our own pioneering research to explore and test out multiple flexible pedagogical approaches that draw on multilingual and multimodal resources in English academic content classrooms.

References

Androutsopoulos, J. (2006) Introduction: Sociolinguistics and computer-mediated communication. *Journal of Sociolinguistics* 10 (4), 419–438.

Androutsopoulos, J. (2007) Bilingualism in the mass media and on the internet. In M. Heller (ed.) *Bilingualism: A Social Approach* (pp. 207–230). Hampshire: Palgrave Macmillan.

Androutsopoulos, J. (2008) Language and the three spheres of hip-hop discourse. In H.S. Alim, A.M. Ibrahim and A. Pennycook (eds) *Global Linguistic Flows: Hip Hop Cultures, Identities, and the Politics of Language* (pp. 43–62). Mahwah, NJ: Lawrence Erlbaum.

Bhatia, V.K. (2001) Analyzing genres: Some conceptual issues. In M. Hewings (ed.) *Academic Writing in Context: Implications and Applications. Papers in Honour of Tony Dudley-Evan* (pp. 79–92). Birmingham: University of Birmingham Press.

Canagarajah, A.S. (ed.) (2005) *Reclaiming the Local in Language Policy and Practice*. Mahwah, NJ: Lawrence Erlbaum.

Cummins, J. (1991) Conversational and academic language proficiency in bilingual contexts. In J.H. Hulstijn and J.F. Matter (eds) *Reading in Two Languages* (pp. 75–89). Amsterdam: AILA.

Davison, C. and Williams, A. (2001) Integrating language and content: Unresolved issues. In B. Mohan, C. Leung and C. Davison (eds) *English as a Second Language in the Mainstream*. Harlow, Essex: Longman (Pearson).

Derewianka, B. (1990) *Exploring How Texts Work*. Newton, NSW: Primary English Teaching Association.

Fang, Z. (2006) The language demands of science reading in middle school. *International Journal of Science Education* 28, 491–520.

Gibbons, P. (1993) *Learning to Learn in a Second Language*. Portsmouth, NH: Heinemann.

Gibbons, P. (2002) *Scaffolding Language, Scaffolding Learning: Teaching Second Language Learners in the Mainstream Classroom*. Portsmouth, NH: Heinemann.

Gibbons, P. (2008) 'It was taught good and I learned a lot': Intellectual practices and ESL learners in the middle years. *Australian Journal of Language and Literacy* 31 (2), 155–173.

Gibbons, P. (2009) *English Learners, Academic Literacy, and Thinking: Learning in the Challenge Zone*. Portsmouth, NH: Heinemann.

Halliday, M.A.K. (1993) *On the Language of Physical Science*. In M.A.K. Halliday and J.R. Martin (eds) *Writing Science: Literacy and Discursive Power* (pp. 54–68). London: Falmer; Pittsburgh: University of Pittsburgh Press (reprinted in Halliday, M.A.K. (2005) *The Language of Science* (pp. 140–158). London: Continuum).

Halliday, M.A.K. (1998) Things and relations: Regrammaticising experience as scientific knowledge. In J.R. Martin and R. Veel (eds) *Reading Science: Critical and Functional Perspectives on Discourse of Science* (pp. 185–235). London: Routledge.

Halliday, M.A.K. (2004) *The Language of Science*. London, New York: Continuum.

Heap, J.L. (1985) Discourse in the production of classroom knowledge: Reading lessons. *Curriculum Inquiry* 15 (3), 245–279.

Hornberger, N. (2003) Multilingual language policies and the continua of biliteracy: An ecological approach. In N.H. Hornberger (ed.) *Continua of Biliteracy: An Ecological*

Framework for Educational Policy, Research, and Practice (pp. 315–339). Clevedon: Multilingual Matters.

Hornberger, N.H. and McKay, S.L. (2010) *Sociolinguistics and Language Education*. Bristol: Multilingual Matters.

Janzen, J. (2008) Teaching English language learners in the content areas. *American Educational Research Association* 78 (4), 1010–1038.

Jones, A. (2007) Immersed twice: How does it work? Proceedings of the Redesigning Pedagogy: Culture, Knowledge and Understanding Conference, Nanyang Technological University, Singapore, 28–30 May.

Kachru, B.B., Kachru, Y. and Nelson, C.L. (eds) (2006) *The Handbook of World Englishes*. Oxford: Blackwell.

Kress, G., Jewitt, C., Ogborn, J. and Tsatsarelis, C. (2001) *Multimodal Teaching and Learning: The Rhetorics of the Science Classroom*. London: Continuum.

Kress, G. and van Leeuwen, T. (1996) *The Grammar of Visual Design*. London: Routledge.

Kress, G. and van Leeuwen, T. (2001) *Multimodal Discourse: The Modes and Media of Contemporary Communication*. London: Arnold.

Lea, M. and Street, B. (1998) Student writing and faculty feedback in higher education: An academic literacies approach. *Studies in Higher Education* 23 (2), 157–172.

Lemke, J.L. (1990) *Talking Science: Language, Learning, and Values*. Norwood, NJ: Ablex Pub. Corp.

Li, D.C.S. (2009) Towards 'biliteracy and trilingualism' in Hong Kong (SAR): Problems, dilemmas and stakeholders' views. *AILA Review* 22, 72–84.

Lillis, T. and Scott, M. (2007) Defining academic literacies research: Issues of epistemology, ideology and strategy. *Journal of Applied Linguistics* 4 (1), 5–32.

Lin, A.M.Y. (1999) Doing-English-lessons in the reproduction or transformation of social worlds? *TESOL Quarterly* 33 (3), 393–412.

Lin, A.M.Y. (2000a) Deconstructing 'mixed code'. In D.C.S. Li, A.M.Y. Lin and W.K. Tsang (eds) *Language and Education in Post-colonial Hong Kong* (pp. 179–194). Hong Kong: Linguistic Society of Hong Kong.

Lin, A.M.Y. (2000b) Resistance and creativity in English reading lessons in Hong Kong. *Language, Culture and Curriculum* 12 (3), 285–296.

Lin, A.M.Y. (2006) Beyond linguistic purism in language-in-education policy and practice: Exploring bilingual pedagogies in a Hong Kong science classroom. *Language and Education* 20 (4), 287–305.

Lin, A.M.Y. (2007) What's the use of 'triadic dialogue'? Activity theory, conversation analysis and analysis of pedagogical practices. *Pedagogies* 2 (2), 77–94.

Lin, A.M.Y. (2008a) 'Respect for da Chopstick Hip Hop': The politics, poetics, and pedagogy of Cantonese verbal art in Hong Kong. In H.S. Alim, A.M. Ibrahim and A. Pennycook (eds) *Global Linguistic Flows: Hip Hop Cultures, Identities, and the Politics of Language* (pp. 159–177). Mahwah, NJ: Lawrence Erlbaum.

Lin, A.M.Y. (2008b) The ecology of literacy in Hong Kong. In A. Creese, P. Martin and N. H. Hornberger (eds) *Encyclopedia of Language and Education, Volume 9: Ecology of Language* (2nd edn) (pp. 291–303). New York: Springer Science.

Lin, A.M.Y. and Man, E.Y.F. (2009) *Bilingual Education: Southeast Asian Perspectives*. Hong Kong: Hong Kong University Press.

Lin, A.M.Y. and Man, E.Y.F. (2011) Doing-hip-hop in the transformation of youth identities: Social class, habitus, and cultural capital. In C. Higgins (ed.) *Negotiating the Self in a Second Language: Identity Formation and Cross-Cultural Adaptation in a Globalizing World* (pp. 201–209). London: Equinox.

Lin, A.M.Y. and Wong, A.S.L. (2011) Science literacy genres in English in Hong Kong junior secondary schools: A pilot project report. Seed Fund Project Report, Faculty of Education, The University of Hong Kong.

Luk, J.C.M. and Lin, A.M.Y. (2005) Uncovering the sociopolitical situatedness of accents in the World Englishes paradigm. In R. Hughes (ed.) *Spoken English, TESOL and Applied Linguistics: Challenges for Theory and Practice* (pp. 3–22). Hampshire: Palgrave Macmillan.

Luke, A., Cazden, C. B., Lin, A.M.Y. and Freebody, P. (2004) *A Coding Scheme for the Analysis of Singapore Classroom Practice*. Singapore: Centre for Research in Pedagogy and Practice, National Institute of Education, Nanyang Technological University.

Martin, J.R. (1989) Technicality and abstraction: Language for the creation of specialised texts. In F. Christie (ed.) *Writing in Schools: Reader* (pp. 36–44). Geelong, Victoria: Deakin University Press (republished in Halliday and Martin, 1993).

Martin, J.R. (1990) Literacy in science: Learning to handle text as technology. In F. Christie (ed.) *Literacy for a Changing World* (pp. 79–117). Melbourne: Australian Council for Educational Research (Fresh Look at the Basics) (republished in Halliday and Martin, 1993: 166–202).

Martin, J.R. (1992) *English Text: System and Structure*. Philadelphia, PA: John Benjamins.

Martin, J.R. (2010) Modelling and mentoring the yin and yang of teaching and learning from home through school. Paper presented at the Faculty of Education, The University of Hong Kong, 10 December.

Martin, J.R. and Painter, C. (ed.) (1986) Writing to mean: Teaching genres across the curriculum (Occasional Papers 9). Sydney, Australia: Applied Linguistics Association of Australia.

Martin, J.R. and Rose, D. (2007) *Working with Discourse: Meaning Beyond the Clause* (2nd edn). London: Continuum (original work published 2003).

Martin, J.R. and Rose, D. (2008) *Genre Relations: Mapping Culture*. London: Equinox.

Mitchell, S. (2006) The Queen Mary Consortium for writing in the disciplines. Thinking writing: News from the Writing in the Disciplines Initiative, Autumn, accessed 28 January 2011. http://www.thinkingwriting.Qmul.ac.uk

Paltridge, B. (2009) *Teaching Academic Writing: An Introduction for Teachers of Second Language Writers*. Ann Arbor: University of Michigan Press.

Paltridge, B. (2012) Teaching English for specific purposes. In A. Burns and J.C. Richards (eds) *The Cambridge Guide to Pedagogy and Practice in Second Language Teaching and Learning* (pp. 179–185). Cambridge: Cambridge University Press.

Pennycook, A. (2003) Global Englishes, Rip Slyme, and performativity. *Journal of Sociolinguistics* 7 (4), 513–533.

Pennycook, A. (2010) *Language as a Local Practice*. London: Routledge.

Prior, P.A. and Hengst, J.A. (eds) (2010) *Exploring Semiotic Remediation as Discourse Practice*. Hampshire: Palgrave Macmillan.

Rees, F. (ed.) (1996) *The Writing Repertoire: Developing Writing at Key Stage 2*. Slough: NFER.

Rose, D. (2008) *Reading to Learn*, accessed 1 September 2010. http://www.readingtolearn.com.au/

Rothery, J. (1990) Story writing in primary school: Assessing narrative type genres. PhD thesis, University of Sydney.

Rothery, J. (1994) *Exploring Literacy in School English (Write it Right Resources for Literacy and Learning)*. Sydney: Metropolitan East Disadvantaged Schools Program.

Rothery, J. (1996) Making changes: Developing an educational linguistics. In R. Hasan and G. Williams (eds) *Literacy in Society* (pp. 86–123). London: Longman.

Russell, D., Lea, M., Parker, J., Street, B. and Donahue, T. (2009) Exploring notions of genre in 'academic literacies' and 'writing in the disciplines': Approaches across countries and contexts. In C. Bazerman, A. Bonini and D. Figueiredo (eds) *Perspectives on Writing* (pp. 395–423). Fort Collins, CO: The WAC Clearinghouse and Parlor Press.

Sinclair, J.M. and Coulthard, R.M. (1975) *Towards an Analysis of Discourse: The English Used by Teachers and Pupils*. London: Oxford University Press.

Street, B.V. (2004) Academic literacies and the 'new orders': Implications for research and practice in student writing in HE. *Learning and Teaching in the Social Sciences* 1 (1), 9–32.

Swales, J.M. (1990) *Genre Analysis: English in Academic and Research Settings*. Cambridge: Cambridge University Press.

Swales, J.M. (2004) *Research Genres: Explorations and Applications*. Cambridge: Cambridge University Press.

6 Multimodal Literacies and Assessment: Uncharted Challenges in the English Classroom

Heather Lotherington and Natalia Sinitskaya Ronda

Introduction

We live in the Canadian province of Ontario where language and literacy share a curriculum for the duration of formal schooling. This conjoined focus, called *Language* in the elementary–junior years, and *English* in the secondary years, epistemologically equates literacy to written English (in English-medium schools). The separate *English as a second language and English literacy development* curriculum in secondary years provides specific remediation towards the regular read-write English language and literacy curriculum. This is school literacy in Ontario; it is standardized, strategically and assiduously assessed, and reported across the full trajectory of compulsory schooling. The approach to literacy taken in our province will resonate in English classrooms in other contexts where literacy is equated to written English. But how did we get to this place?

Modern mass schooling, which forms the base for contemporary educational design, gained momentum in the 19th century, moving towards a factory model of vernacular literacy and away from classical premises, including the use of Latin as the medium of education. But as the world has grown more populous, more traversable and more internally connected in a parallel digital universe, 20th-century values of alphabetic print literacy and standard English, and their associated competency frameworks, have become a poor fit for contemporary communication practices.

We live in global times. Our technologies of communication enable multiple modalities that reach out to and connect global populations instantaneously. Though English has emerged as a lingua mundi, and the focus on transcribed English as key to the world of print is still a fundamental, acquiring proficient written English is insufficient for full participation in the literate world of today. The familiar parameters of accuracy and fluency in language use (only selectively assessable in literacy tests) require other dimensions now to capture complementary and hybridized modes of expression, dynamic texts and participatory authorship structures.

However, the shift towards multiple, interlinked modes of communication is not very apparent in the archival world of school literacies – certainly in the case of the English classrooms we describe here – which has been resistant to change, continuing to function largely on paper, and limiting access to digital mediation which amplifies and extends multimodal capacities. Though experimental literacy interventions using multiple modes of communication and digital mediation have been implemented on a project basis in English classrooms around the globe (e.g. Dooley, 2008; and Tan & McWilliam, 2009: English as an Additional Language students in Australia; Lotherington, 2011: elementary school children in Canada; Tan *et al.*, 2010: high school students in Singapore), and in after-school projects (e.g. Ware & Warschauer, 2005, a university–community digital storytelling program in California), systemic change in language and literacy education has lagged sadly behind. As Lankshear and Knobel (2006: 30) remark:

> What seems to be happening is that the day-to-day business of school is still dominated by conventional literacies, and engagement with the 'new' literacies is largely confined to learners' lives in spaces outside of schools and other formal educational settings.

A conservative force working against change in language and literacy education is the standardized test, which answers to demands for accountability in education, but is cued to modern literacy practices. In the case of Ontario, literacy – understood as written English – is tested in Grades 3, 6 and 10 by the Education Quality and Accountability Office (EQAO), which was set up by the provincial conservative government of the mid-1990s (ETFO, 2011), following the American educational model which began to incorporate standardized testing in the early 20th century (Spolsky, 1995). Menken (2008) explains that in the United States where no official national language is legislated, standardized language testing has historically formed a central component of language policy. The EQAO is further linked to American educational values in that it was field-tested in coordination with the American giant, Educational Testing Services (ETS) (EQAO, 2009), which administers over 50 million tests in 180 countries (ETS, 2011), including influential tests of English language proficiency, such as the Test of English as a Foreign Language (TOEFL).

Contemporary communication practices offer serious challenges to modern conceptions of literacy: the page is no longer the predominant site of literacy; text is no longer static or necessarily print-centered; literate production may be collaborative, confronting the historic assignation of authorship and authority to the individual (e.g. copyright); and prescriptive grammar, canonical spelling and sentence mechanics no longer equate to literacy achievement.

It is time to rethink the borders of contemporary communication – how it is conceptualized, taught and assessed in the English classroom. In this era, written English has developed alternative standards in, for example, texting (see Crystal, 2008; Lotherington & Xu, 2004; Tagliamonte & Denis, 2008; Thurlow & Brown, 2003), and English is undergoing rapid changes in global use. Speech and writing, as conceived in school curricula, find limited, partial, complementary, complex and hybridized roles in cyberspace, where the semiotic means for communicating fundamentally include image, font, layout, sound and animation, as in a website. Digital communication is fluid, multimodal and increasingly less reliant on textual information, depending on a complex mesh of visual, spatial and audio semiotic means. So how far does a test of prescriptive English grammar go in tapping these new ways with words?

Literacy and Multimodality

The concept of *multiliteracies* inspired thought about 'the multiplicity of communications channels and media, and the increasing salience of cultural and linguistic diversity' (New London Group, 1996: 63) in the emerging world order of the late 20th century. The concept of *mode* is key in the move from conceptions of *literacy* as reading and writing (English), to awareness of *multiliteracies* that take account of multiple media plus cultural and linguistic diversity, to delineations of *multimodal literacies* that incorporate multiple semiotic resources in complex configurations. *Mode* is defined by Kress (2009: 54) as 'a socially shaped and culturally given resource for making meaning. *Image, writing, layout, music, gesture, speech, moving image, soundtrack* are examples of modes used in representation and communication'. Multimodal literacies, then, merge multiple modes of communication, which include reading and writing within a larger panorama of expressive channels; for instance, a video-sharing site such as YouTube connects moving images and sound with textual commentary. Classroom literacy teaching and assessment tend to ignore or simply miss these convergent information channels in their focus on reading and writing print.

Multimodality is a concomitant of human communication. Speech consists not only of vocalization, but also gesture, facial expression and the physical distance between speakers. We strip away this rich multisensory tapestry when archiving conversation, no matter which technology has been selected for conservation – audio recording, photographic reproduction, illustration or alphabetic transcription. Even video recording loses contextual ambience that contributes to how the listener attends to the talk.

Nor is multimodality a new phenomenon in printed text. This is magnificently exemplified in early illuminated manuscripts.[1] Nishimura (2009) delineates the humans, animals and hybrid creatures that are living and playing in the decorative borders of medieval illuminated manuscripts, illustrating the stories that are being revealed in subtextual spaces. Figure 6.1 depicts a

Figure 6.1 *Queen Mary Psalter* by Unknown Miniaturist, English (circa 1310)[2]

page of a 14th-century illuminated British manuscript, which includes a narrative embedded in a majuscule.

Many texts are fundamentally bimodal, juxtaposing alphabetic print and image: a children's picture book, a recipe book, an atlas; some are multimodal: a mathematics text that utilizes words and numbers as well as charts, diagrams, formulae and so on, or a *National Geographic* magazine[3] that uses alphabetic print, photographs and maps; but others are essentially monomodal, such as the novel, though it can be justifiably argued that visual design (e.g. layout, font) is also at play here. In education we have gradually focused in on written language to the exclusion of other modes of communication. In mandatory literacy tests in Ontario, created and administered by the EQAO, reading and writing are assessed in terms of the grammatical, spelling and punctuation conventions of encoding, such that the commas seem to matter more than the content.

Multimodal literacies are not limited to the English classroom; they describe new communicative trends in language generally. However, the research reported here, including the historical galvanization of multiliteracies as a new direction in literacy and language education is based in and on classrooms where English is the focus of attention.

Multimodality and Digital Mediation

Twenty-first century literacies, we would argue, include both linguistic and extralinguistic meaning-making resources unrecognizable in literacy instruction only a decade ago. Bezemer and Kress (2008) point out that not only are there now more images in texts, which look and function in new ways, but that 'modes of representation other than image and writing – moving image and speech for instance – have found their way into learning resources, with significant effect' (Bezemer & Kress, 2008: 167).

Multiple modes of expression can be merged using digital tools to create a text that is no longer static. This digitally manipulable, multimodal text is dynamic: it has *read/write* possibility rather than the *read only* function of a paper text. Jewitt (2002: 183) explains, 'new technologies offer the potential to "recast modes" in ways which blur the boundaries between the visual and the written'. Cope and Kalantzis (2009: 361) extrapolate:

> After half a millennium or longer in which written text was a pervasive source of knowledge and power, photographic means of representation (lithographic printing, cinema, analogue television) began to afford greater power to image and comfortably overlay image with written text.

The digital accelerates this process as the elementary modular unit of manufacture of textual meaning is reduced from the character to the pixel. Images and fonts are now made of the same raw materials.

The fundamental shift in the minimal encoding unit from letter to pixel (Cope & Kalantzis, 2009) profoundly challenges our notion of literacy as decoding and encoding alphabetic print according to fixed conventions, and offers a virtually endless landscape of representational possibilities: from images and sounds to augmented and virtual reality. This shift calls for a revisiting of the essential literacy toolkit. Moving away from a narrow understanding of literacy as reading and writing English print, we must deal with the changing and shifting realities of the pixelized world: how are meanings conveyed across multiple media? How are they *written* and *read* in multiple modes?

Contemporary multiple modes operate in networked spaces; they are social, collaborative, dynamic, interactive, multimodal, transmodal, glocal and hybridized. They have produced new genres, venues, discourses, identities, participatory modes, thinking spaces and authorial practices in, for example, class website construction combining wikis, blogs and videos. Digitally-mediated multimodal practices require more freedom than expected or available in modern top-down educational systems that exert curricular control, promote transmission models of information access and limit discursive and collaborative possibilities online. They also require new assessment mechanisms.

Teaching and Assessing Multimodal Literacies: Conflicts and Disjunctures

A substantial roadblock to educational reform is the creeping externalization of assessment bodies, which have transmogrified from 'a cottage industry to big business' (Spolsky, 2008: 301) in which control has moved from classroom teachers and educationists to big business. The EQAO, which was put into place by a former conservative provincial government, works behind closed doors to construct consequential tests of literacy acquisition according to their interpretation of curricular documents. These test makers do not interactively include teachers or tap quotidian classroom practices in their test development to the chagrin of classroom teachers who must prepare their children to participate in a test that does not take into account what they have actually done in class. Divorcing learning from assessment has consequences in multiple directions: it affects the shape of public reporting measures and the social values they engender; it influences school and teacher recognition models and hiring practices by rewarding those who perform well on external assessments; it encourages teaching towards the test in the classroom, which favors transmission and coaching models; and it redirects the emphasis in teacher education programs towards the skills tapped in tests.

Classroom teachers are positioned to unwittingly hamper the development of multimodal literacies and learning in the classroom where an external test is the final determinant of successful language and literacy learning. Tan *et al.* (2010: 6) point out: 'it is naïve to assume that new literacies will spontaneously thrive in the ordinary English classroom just because of the impact of the digital age or new times', stressing that the teacher is a crucial link in instituting multimodal practices in the classroom. To understand the meta-language of contemporary multimodal practices and implement them in the English classroom, particularly where they are navigating environments that are politically constrained by traditional assessment procedures, teachers need professional support and development. Tan *et al.* (2010) offer a case in point in Singapore, where a secondary school teacher was resistant to veering away from the traditional expectations of the English classroom that are tested in paper-based examinations despite her school's expressed vision of instituting a transformative critical multiliteracies approach. As a participant in an exploratory case project implementing multimodal practices in high school English teaching, the teacher grew in her understanding of meaning-making, and expanded her classroom practices to include multimodal texts, but 'remained adamant about critical multimedia literacies being less important than conventional literacy' (Tan *et al.*, 2010: 14), though she saw the multimodal practices as contributing towards *examinable skills*.

Creative contemporary multimodal literacies challenge existing educational structures that continue to rely on the top-down, authoritative and prescribed model of knowledge transmission from teacher to students, aptly labeled the *banking model of education* by Paulo Freire (2000). The creative, fluid and collaborative nature of new digital media invite a revitalized pedagogical vision that includes paradigms of collaborative, multimodal, shared, multiplatform, social learning, which Gee (2010: 14) argues compellingly for:

> The emerging area of digital media and learning is not just the study of how digital tools can enhance learning. It is, rather, the study of how digital tools and new forms of convergent media, production, and participation, as well as powerful forms of social organization and complexity in popular culture, can teach us how to enhance learning in and out of school and how to transform society and the global world as well.

Whereas the rapid evolution of mobile technologies does not automatically enable participatory thinking, it certainly challenges the fixedness of context and community in learning. Bo-Kristensen and Meyer (2008) track how networking and mobility have shifted authority from the text to the teacher to the hands of students with technological development. Their genealogy of contemporary digital technologies used in second and foreign language teaching contexts starts with the 1950s language lab – a fixed class space outfitted with tape-based audio equipment designed to facilitate and support language acquisition – moving to the digital lab, which reduced the traditional formality of the classroom by inviting audiovisual immediacy into lessons, to the era of portable devices such as smart phones, which permit learners to capture their own content for sharing in class, giving the learner the agency to contribute authentic material to their own language learning, and enabling a participatory culture in the development of language resources. This *agency* is not acknowledged or utilized in externally developed tests, which place authority firmly outside of the student, the teacher and the classroom in the hands of the test maker.

In the new digital media paradigm, particularly striking are examples of self-organized knowledge communities: learning has increasingly gone grassroots, social and in terms of access, global. Wikipedia, a collaboratively edited multilingual digital encyclopedia, serves as a stark reminder that knowledge and learning can be popular, community-oriented, collaborative and self-organized. While Wikipedia is regarded with suspicion and even outward hostility in educational institutions, it offers important opportunities for learning about community-centered creation, collaboration, editing, legitimacy and authority in knowledge production, dissemination and publishing.

The digital gap that once existed in children's access to hardware has virtually closed in North America. But what young people do with the technology they access is another issue. Access to technology does not necessarily lead to critical use: education has a central role to play in analyzing and incorporating contemporary technologies of communication. Socially, today's teenagers routinely access varied media for fun, and the digital paths they take inevitably vary. While their social literacy practices (e.g. Facebook, YouTube, fanfiction, videogaming) are varied in breadth and depth – we can no longer equate age with digital proficiency (Bennett *et al.*, 2008) – their social networking and gaming practices are rarely validated as significant or valuable in formal educational settings. In school, students' use of the internet is tightly controlled, and their use of social media, highly restricted. Jenkins (2009) points out that by sanctioning some digital practices and discouraging others, current educational structures are increasing the participation gap, generating unequal opportunities to engage meaningfully with new technologies. He explains that increasing access to digital tools will only successfully close the gap when 'coupled with new educational initiatives to help youths and adults learn how to use those tools effectively' (Jenkins, 2009: 17).

Multimodal Literacies in the English Classroom: Two Examples

We each began experimental forays into multimodal literacies in the school classroom by working on an interventionist basis in collaboration with established and experienced teachers interested in instituting change in literacy pedagogy. The Toronto school populations with which we are working comprise children born in the digital age in 175 different countries. These children are culturally and linguistically conversant in digital genres (including maintaining profiles on social networks, producing and uploading digital images and multimedia, and engaging in digital communication via text messaging and instant communication), which form a social bridge across their diverse physical and linguistic cultural experiences.

We now report on two school interventions to develop multimodal literacies in the Toronto area – one in elementary school, and one in secondary school.

Distributed learning in Grade 4/5 special education: *The Window Woman* DVD

Rhea Perreira-Foyle's Grade 4/5 class (i.e. children aged 8–10) at Joyce Public School[4] is special education; it includes children with a range of diagnosed learning difficulties, most of whom are also English as a Second Language (ESL) learners. Rhea has been a long-term collaborator in a school–university action research project that has been in existence since 2003, devoted to the development of multimodal literacies pedagogies[5] (see Lotherington, 2009, 2011). The participating teachers and researchers in this collaborative project have formed a *learning community* committed to developing innovative project-based approaches to teaching language and literacy that include children's knowledge of community languages, and digital pop culture practices. Classroom projects are designed by participating teachers with researchers from York University; each annual project targets specific curricular aims and crosses disciplines, age groups, languages and abilities to engage children in the active creation of focused multimodal narratives. The participating teachers have specific investments in developing multimodal literacies: Rhea is successfully engaging children with diagnosed learning problems that make learning to read and write in English particularly challenging.

In Rhea's project: *The Window Woman*, the children engaged in multiple activities culminating in the creation of a video that was inspired by the juvenile novel, *The Breadwinner* (Ellis, 2000). The novel is about a young Afghan girl who disguises herself as a boy and leaves home to find food for her starving family after her father is taken prisoner by the Taliban. It is a story about courage and resourcefulness in a repressed society where unescorted females are confined to the home by law. Rhea's social justice agenda drew on the novel's depiction of barbaric social revisionism, focusing particularly on repressive sexism.

Rhea's plan for the children took them through a careful reading of the novel, which is a slow procedure for children with multiple learning challenges coupled with ESL backgrounds. This is where the traditional English classroom begins and all too frequently ends. But for Rhea's children, this was only the beginning of a multimodal journey. While they read the novel, the children cross-dressed in culturally appropriate Muslim garb so they could feel what it was like to wear clothes that marked them as free to walk on the street in the context of the novel – or not. Initially, the boys showed considerable resistance to wearing women's clothing (and some parents complained), but eventually all settled into wearing a hijab while they read the book, which helped them to empathize with the cultural reality of the characters they were studying.

A character in Ellis' novel that is not well developed is a woman who reports on what she sees from a window. The class identified her as *the window woman*, and built a story about the novel from her point of view. This is a sophisticated undertaking in Grade 4/5 special education, reminiscent of Tom Stoppard's (1967) play, *Rosencrantz and Guildenstern Are Dead*, which builds an existential story around the scripted lives of two minor characters left hanging in Shakespeare's play, *The Tragedy of Hamlet, Prince of Denmark*. The children scripted the story as seen from the vantage point of the window woman, and reinterpreted the lives of the people she describes in short vignettes. These acted scenarios were videotaped and narrated for inclusion in the final class multimodal product, which they opted to do in a television talk show format.

Upon reading Sawyer's (2006) stance on learning as creativity, which was a recommended resource shared in our learning community, Rhea decided to try out his observation that 'the most effective classroom discussion has the free-flowing collaborativeness of an improvisational theater performance' (Sawyer, 2006: 44). She gave the students the administrative freedom to put together the final multimodal product of their learning, stepping back from her directorial role as teacher. The class had to make executive decisions amongst themselves about who should direct, who should interview, how scenes should be shot and how the audience should act. The director's cut programmed the videotaped flashbacks of the characters' lives into the final DVD to flesh out the talk show chats.

The responsibility for each contributing role in the project was assumed on a volunteer basis. Rhea reports, comically, that she was on the verge of panic watching the chaos as children tried to sort out who should do what in their talk show. Some children elected to take on particular roles; others assumed a position in the pretend television studio audience. Allowing the children to choose their own roles revealed surprises. For example, a boy who would not speak in class spontaneously picked up the difficult task of video-editing. A young girl diagnosed as mildly intellectually impaired demonstrated the role of the talk show host to her fellow students, giving an electrifying performance, after which the children insisted she continue. The final DVD presentation was a collage of first-person talk show interviews and biographical back stories, narrated in English with a Pashto introduction. The children took charge of their production, and had fun doing so.

On viewing the final DVD production, the teachers admitted to astonishment at the accomplishment of children who were labeled low academic performers with diagnosed learning problems, and, predominantly, ESL backgrounds. Their multimodal literacy project involved:

- *reading* an English language juvenile novel (with a great deal of specialist help and encouragement);
- *studying* point of view;
- *retelling* the story from an alternate viewpoint;
- *researching* and *embodying* the lived reality of the characters in terms of dress;
- *creating* a talk show based on the novel's cast of characters;
- *compiling*;
- *scripting*; and
- *acting* the back stories of the characters;
- *performing* a talk show presentation to interview the characters of the novel;
- *videotaping* the flashbacks, and the show; and
- *video-editing* their DVD project (see Figures 6.2 and 6.3 for screenshots from the DVD).

Figure 6.2 Screenshot of talk show from *The Window Woman*

Figure 6.3 Screenshot of autobiographical flashback from *The Window Woman*

The work was interpretive, research-based and creative. The learning model was collaborative, self-directed and multimodal, involving narrative and scripted text, acting, costume preparation and video capture, and allowing those with problems accessing text to engage other supportive means of expression. Importantly for children with diagnosed learning problems, the learning was distributed so that all children did not have to have the same *skill* level, but could contribute different pieces to the whole project. This learning model works creatively with what children *can do* rather than punitively testing them on what they *cannot do*. These were Rhea's special education learners: a group of low achievers with multiple problems in accessing written English, streamed into remedial education on the basis of their scores on standardized tests.

How will these students' language and literacy learning be assessed?

The English language and literacy skills of the children in Rhea's Grade 4/5 special education class will be assessed in Grade 6 along with all other Grade 6 children in the province of Ontario by the Education Quality and Accountability Office (EQAO), whose test questions and scoring rubrics are available online (EQAO, 2010). Two booklets of questions are given to students during different test periods; together they tap a limited range of *literacy skills* on paper: reading prose and poetry passages across cultural and scientific topics with attendant comprehension and vocabulary questions; and writing short descriptive essays and instructions as well as answering multiple choice questions on punctuation and grammar.

The 2009–2010 test 1 reading passages include a text on Caleb and Aidan playing hockey, a poem on dogsleds and a piece on Gordon Lightfoot, a popular Canadian folksinger of the 1960s and 1970s. These topics, which are laden with Canadian symbolism, give little opportunity for children of culturally diverse backgrounds living in a large metropolitan area (in this century) to engage background knowledge. The majority of children at Joyce Public School speak English as a second language,[6] and will struggle with multiple choice questions on English vocabulary and grammar, such as:

The word 'shambled' as used in line 10 means

(a) Moved clumsily.
(b) Climbed quickly.
(c) Walked carefully.
(d) Marched proudly. (EQAO, 2010: 8)

For the children in Rhea's class, who have learning challenges, ESL issues and, as recent immigrants to Canada, limited cultural capital, this test, which requires the same knowledge base and performance level from each student, tested individually, will be a self-confirming exercise in failure. As their complex multimodal DVD project on *The Breadwinner* indicates, they are capable of complex, creative work that is not tapped in limited standardized assessment vehicles. Given the opportunity to work with a creative mandate in a group, the children far exceeded the expectations of their teachers. Their collaborative literacy achievement is, however, not tapped in EQAO multiple choice and constrained essay questions, completed individually. We argue that EQAO literacy testing is unfairly limited, and unsupportive of these children's educational success.

Socially networked multimodal literacy in a Grade 11 English class: Facebook

Marjory Veller[7] teaches a Grade 11 (i.e. adolescents aged ~16–17) university preparation English course in a large urban high school in Toronto. While Marjory's course fits into the broader secondary *English* curriculum, she has focused primarily on composition, engaging her students with a variety of texts and media, including blogs and YouTube videos. As part of the course, students studied the novel *Their Eyes Were Watching God* (Hurston, 1937/1991) set in the United States in the early 20th century, featuring a female African American protagonist.

The students enrolled in Marjory's course are linguistically and culturally diverse. Many arrived in Canada as children or teenagers; others can be described as generation 1.5 learners – students who were born in Canada to immigrant parents and share characteristics of both the home and the host cultures (Harklau *et al.*, 1999). In their social lives this group of adolescent learners is engaged with a variety of digital media that support their glocal social and educational engagement. They choose digital tools that allow them to mirror and extend their physical social connections, and benefit from opportunities to communicate and find resources online. They are developing competencies and literacies that focus on connecting, socializing, communicating and researching in the digital world. These teens have many digital tools at their fingertips: from YouTube for researching the different recitations of the Qur'an, to an online social network in their first language to facilitate their connection with friends back home. They accept or reject these tools based on the social meanings they construct with them.

Facebook, a popular social networking site, serves as a space of digital socialization for these teens, and many practices that these adolescents are engaged in online support their literacy and language development. Their experiences with Facebook are rich in language use and meaning-making possibilities. By engaging in different media and genres of textual and multimedia production on Facebook, these teens learn important lessons about voice, genre, tone, audience, expressiveness – all indispensable competencies in a literacy curriculum. These teens have learned to navigate the text heavy environment of Facebook, engage in reading and writing in new digital genres, including status updates and notes, and work out new rules for engaging with friends through multimedia. They are immersed in a multimodal communication environment, with access to virtually limitless digital bricks (e.g. notes, links, photos, videos, groups, applications, profiles) with which to construct their space, and themselves within their space.

The research project offered Marjory an opportunity to bring Facebook, a space of informal sociality for students, into their formal engagement with language and literacy. For the purposes of this study an application was developed on the Facebook platform with three different environments to support students' learning in the course:

- *stories* offered a space for the students to share their individual writing, and facilitated commenting from peers;
- *videos* allowed students to upload clips from YouTube and provide annotations; and
- *wikis* were a space for collaborative writing, where all students could contribute and edit any contribution.

Marjory integrated the application into her instruction of *Their Eyes Were Watching God*, and called on particular digital tools in the Facebook environment for two assignments. Students posted descriptive paragraphs from individual compositions they wrote in the course, which were then critiqued by their peers. Videos and wikis supported students' research objectives, helping them form a critical understanding of the historical context of the novel they were studying. Students in groups created wikis on a research topic proposed by Marjory, additionally submitting individual videos to provide further background for their research topic.

Students were familiar with both academic writing within the school setting, and informal digital writing on social networks; in this project they were presented with an opportunity to blend the two. In posting a sample of their writing on the Facebook application, where they gave and received peer feedback, they found they could share their ideas. The students felt inspired by reading their classmates' contributions, which had previously been largely for the teacher's eyes only.

Videos allowed students to tap into the multimodal potential of the Facebook application, and produce meaning in diverse formats. Students applied a range of competencies to this task: doing online research, classifying and connecting knowledge in meaningful ways, finding and uploading videos, tagging, and writing up a description that makes salient their emergent understanding of the topic. While many students opted for instructional or documentary videos that provided a background for the historical context of the novel, one student tapped into popular culture to find connections between the early 20th-century United States and contemporary teenage culture. Alia selected a video featuring a rap song focusing on the Harlem Renaissance (see Figure 6.4).

The wiki creation facilitated a collaborative writing activity in which small groups of learners did research and contributed to a wiki on a particular topic that supported their novel study. This introduced an important digital paradigm to their learning: writing and knowing collaboratively. While group work is encouraged in Marjory's class, the wiki collaboration gave students a new perspective on writing digitally. As one student put it, 'when you are doing like a group activity, and you're all at one desk, and one person usually has the pen and paper, everyone gives the idea and then one person writes it. So you can't get your full idea across. But in the wiki you can just edit it, so it's kind of like everyone has a piece

Figure 6.4 Video submitted by Alia on the topic of the Harlem Renaissance

of that paper'. Some students elected to submit an individual rather than a collaborative wiki. This may reflect the curricular emphasis on individual assessment which does not assign a collaborative grade to collaborative tasks.

How will these students' language and literacy learning be assessed?

In Toronto, the Ontario Secondary School Literacy Test (OSSLT) is the arbiter of literacy acquisition in secondary school education. Given to students across the province in Grade 10, the OSSLT tests 'essential reading and writing skills that apply to all subject areas in the provincial curriculum up to the end of Grade 9'.[8] The definition of literacy adopted by the external agency responsible for the OSSLT, the EQAO, comprises 'the reading and writing skills required to understand reading selections and communicate through a variety of written forms as expected in *The Ontario Curriculum* across all subjects' (EQAO, 2007: 5). This definition has not changed since the OSSLT was introduced in 2002 (Radwan *et al.*, 2010).

Paradoxically, by firmly grounding the concept of literacy within 'reading and writing skills', the EQAO's mandate is at odds with the Ontario curriculum, which promotes a much broader understanding of literacy:

> Literacy development is a communal project, and the teaching of literacy skills is embedded across the Ontario curriculum. However, it is the English curriculum that is dedicated to developing the knowledge and skills on which literacy is based – that is, knowledge and skills in the areas of listening and speaking, reading, writing, and viewing and representing. (Ontario Ministry of Education, 2007: 3)

Though the Ontario curriculum envisages literacy in terms of skills, the extension of the traditional four skills model (reading-writing-listening-speaking) to include viewing and representing invites multimodal activities, involving modal complexity and dynamic textual transformation.

Externally driven, psychometrically oriented models of summative literacy assessment typically focus on prose literacy, document literacy and quantitative literacy (Gal, 2002; Freebody & Lo Bianco, 1997; Watson & Callingham, 2003), following the influential work of Kirsch *et al.* (1998), whose conceptual delineation of the three interrelated concepts underpinning *literacy* created the basis for national literacy surveys in Canada, the United States and Australia, as well as large-scale literacy studies, most notably, the International Adult Literacy Survey, conducted by the Organisation for Economic Co-operation and Development (OECD) (Gal, 2002).

Gal (2002: 8) notes that document literacy was identified as primary outside of school settings where prose literacy predominates, explaining:

> Document literacy tasks require people to identify, interpret, and use information given in lists, tables, indexes, schedules, charts and graphic displays. The information in such displays often includes explicit quantitative information, such as numbers or percents, in addition to the quantitative or statistical information conveyed in such charts.

The characterization of literacy as a set of specific cognitive skills 'required to locate information in documents, and ... match information in a question or directive to corresponding information in arrays of varying degrees of complexity' (Gal, 2002: 8) is a poor fit for socially embedded multimodal literacies, which vary, essentially, in nature, scope and process. The epistemological premise that a single score could capture the creative dimensions of literate learning is utterly untenable. Yet, a single score on the multidimensional ability to negotiate the textual world in all its complexity is exactly what the OSSLT delivers (Radwan *et al.*, 2010).

The students who experienced learning through Facebook valued opportunities to engage with a community of learners: sharing their thoughts and their writing with peers and giving and receiving feedback, finding a voice through multimodal means, and writing collaboratively. In testing mechanisms, such as the OSSLT, this collaborative learning is invalidated, student voice being secondary to conventional use of grammar, spelling and sentence mechanics; and students' expertise with digital multimedia along with their personal interests, rendered irrelevant. The OSSLT emphasizes individual performance on a prescribed and inauthentic test, thus stripping away students' growing confidence in themselves as competent writers and communicators, taking away their audience, and removing the digital tools for meaning-making with which they are familiar.

New Parameters for Language and Literacy Assessment

Students today live in a rich, diverse, digitally mediated cultural space, but the literacy practices they engage in socially are not recognized in the gatekeeping, standardized literacy tests affecting learners of English that assume a conception of literacy as a portable cognitive skill, and texts as static, universally interpretable documents (on paper in English). Students are, thus, internalizing discourses that their extracurricular multimodal practices are not valid, relevant or valuable. However, multimodal practices developing in social forums in digital space offer their users new challenges, new content and new ways to engage and interact with text, creating new possibilities for classroom learning.

We can look to user engagement in social networking, fanfiction and interactive gaming sites, to name a few, to discover working models of how to engage and refashion educational content, and how to take a problem, work out and customize solutions. Bringing multimodal practices into class-room learning demands a revised model for assessment that moves away from standardized measures of individual written performance in English, and towards multimodal, multiplatform, collaborative and socially authentic forms of assessment.

Literacy practices in the English classroom have changed dimensionally. Historically applicable external language and literacy testing procedures relate poorly to contemporary dynamic texts, the tools used to produce them and the collaborative and distributed authorship structures enabled in their pro-duction. Fundamental to this mind shift is a consideration of new *basics* in communication and education, and new borders in learning environments.

New basics

Assessment backlashes often demand going back to basics. But the basics have changed. New literacy practices that have grown in new media environ-ments have inspired new pedagogies, new ways of learning and new intel-lectual products. So what are the *new* basics?

Sinclair (2010) rewrites the traditional *three Rs* of modern education: *Reading, wRiting, aRithmetic* as *four Rs* for a digital era in which information is recombinant: *Reuse* (backup), *Revise* (adapt), *Remix* (combine), *Redistribute* (share). These new basics describe creating, processing and distributing infor-mation in contemporary convergence culture (Jenkins, 2006), involving dynamism, collaboration and multimodality. Though formal education still provides a curriculum based on factual knowledge, this knowledge base must be treated as more fluid – constructed and shared in dynamic and collabora-tive ways. So how could this be assessed?

Kalantzis and Cope (2008: ¶3) offer a big picture of six core principles for a new agenda in assessment that 'builds on identity and social cognition, builds meta-cognition, is ubiquitous, offers formative assessment, promotes authentic learning, and uses multimodal texts' (see http://newlearningonline. com/news/assess-as-you-go/). This elaborated focus challenges the modern-ist agenda of universal and unflinching linguistically described standards, shifting arbitration of literacy learning from static summative testing of language structure and information retrieval to ongoing, dynamic, socially invested, multimodal action.

The project of dismantling the old basics of reading and writing alphabetic print according to historico-cultural conventions involves the recognition and promulgation of a paradigm that describes the digitally mediated, multimodal competencies needed to locate, critically draw out, link (i.e. *read*), and create, construct and disseminate (i.e. *write*) meaningful discourse for authentic purposes. These new basics are less concerned with conventional correctness and individual performance, and more with multimodal expressiveness and appropriateness, dynamic collaboration and the utilization of emerging sociality. Consider *new basics* to include:

- *Multimodality*: multiple modes of representation and expression in complex interplay.
- *Multimedia*: mediating technologies; multiple platforms.
- *Connectivity*: local and global issues, participants.
- *Collaboration*: sociality; networks; shared authorship.
- *Dynamism*: customizability; transmodality; transmediality; impermanence.
- *Hybridity*: mixing and remixing old-new content, forms, genres, media.

New borders in learning environments

Borders around learning spaces have been expanded to include learners of diverse cultural, linguistic and learning backgrounds. Though this is a patent reality in the contemporary urban classroom, we must extend our thinking beyond the bricks-and-mortar classroom. School walls can be permeated digitally; learners can connect and collaborate online. With global online communities growing in online social networks, classrooms, too, can be re-imagined as global communities.

The digitally networked classroom creates new communities of learners who may be localized in different physical learning environments. Arguably, *lingua franca English* more aptly describes the language that learners of English acquire (Canagarajah, 2007) than *standard English* in contemporary global communication. The digitally mediated multimodal literacies they engage in extend and augment their:

- *social investment*: complex identity-formation; and
- *authentic engagement*: social reach and impact.

Assessment must, in turn, move from focusing on idealized notions of standard language correctness and static information retrieval to communicative facility in real communities of practice that may extend across linguistic and cultural borders in digital space. How can this be done?

Towards Assessment of Multimodal Literacies

Local classroom engagement, amplified and reinforced digitally, becomes *glocal*. Students can participate in projects that engage them locally in their community to produce real-world outcomes. Examples range from local interest groups (e.g. http://www.facebook.com/home.php#!/group.php?gid=92647291523&v) to high school election campaigns on Facebook (e.g. http://www.facebook.com/group.php?gid=328030391580) to multilateral projects shared across collaborative teams of teachers, students and schools (http://www.multiliteracies4kidz.ca; http://www.multiliteracies.ca/). Educational assessment approaches real-world assessment, asking, 'What impact has this communication made?' A positive outcome for the local community becomes a critical measure of success.

Assessment of learners' projects can be guided by the basic principles set out by Kalantzis and Cope (2008), which fundamentally include formative assessment, multimodality and digital access. Assessment would ask whether and how the activity:

- builds on identity and social cognition?
- builds meta-cognition?
- promotes authentic learning?

Literacy engagement in project-based learning can be considered in terms of the new basics we set out in this chapter:

- *Multimodality*: How are modes used to convey meaning?
- *Multimedia*: What mediating technologies are used, how and why?
- *Connectivity*: What issues and participants are engaged, why and how?
- *Collaboration*: How is textual creation/learning distributed?
- *Dynamism*: How and why is this text customized?
- *Hybridity*: How are old-new elements engaged?

Where do new digital tools fit into language and literacy assessment in the English classroom? The availability and diversity of digital media pose an interesting challenge to computer-assisted assessment. The future of computer- and mobile-assisted assessment may be based on a form of artificial intelligence: a learning computer that can adapt and modify input depending on the individual learner.[9] But in light of rising digital connectivity and socialization trends, the best application for digital tools in assessment is the expansion and amplification of the learning community: assessment taken out of the realm of the individual and the prescribed, and thrown into the unpredictable and messy, but authentic and social, digital community assessment model. Such assessment might include digital portfolios that are completed individually and in various groupings, physical and virtual, then assessed by educators and outside experts.

As we enter the second decade of the 21st century, McLuhan's (1962) vision of a *post-typographic* era in which print is no longer the medium of power has become a reality. The digitally mediated multimodal communication we engage in on a quotidian basis to interconnect the worlds of atoms and bits we inhabit (Negroponte, 1995) has changed not only our structures of participation and engagement, but, increasingly, our consciousness, as, for example, *to friend* becomes a verb, and global conversations are *invited* or, conversely, *blocked*. The challenges in bringing our pedagogies and assessment practices up to date, though clearly challenging, may have as much to do with political recognition of the inadequate fit of current classroom language and literacy teaching and testing to 21st-century communication practices as navigating uncharted pedagogical waters. Politically invested agencies, such as the EQAO, cannot continue unopposed to base their consequential tests on old research and old definitions of literacy that functionally guard 20th-century structuralism. Arbiters of literacy success must link classroom learning to real social communication needs and possibilities. Imagination and energy are needed to assess dynamic multimodal literacies appropriately. But in a communicative world where virtual basics and glocal learning communities are driving exciting new horizons in learning one thing is certain: we cannot continue to make judgments of this learning based on individual paper tests of standard English grammar and information retrieval from static documents.

Notes

(1) The British Library has many of its rare medieval manuscripts available for viewing online. The catalogue of illuminated manuscripts with explanations of their characteristics is available at: http://www.bl.uk/catalogues/illuminatedmanuscripts/GlossA.asp.

(2) Image from the public domain available under the Creative Commons Attribution/Share-Alike License retrieved from http://commons.wikimedia.org/wiki/File:Queen_Mary%27s_Psalter.jpg.

(3) See: http://www.nationalgeographic.com/.

(4) The Principal of Joyce Public School and the teachers who are reported here have requested that their real names and the real name of the school be used, and have signed informed consent forms to allow this. All children remain anonymous.

(5) We acknowledge with gratitude the Social Sciences and Humanities Research Council for their continuing support of our research. Rhea's classroom project was completed as part of a standard research grant to Heather Lotherington and Jennifer Jenson, entitled: *Researching New Literacies in the Multicultural Classroom: Developing a Ludic Approach to Linguistic Challenges in Elementary Education.*

(6) Approximately two-thirds of the children at Joyce Public School speak a language other than English at home; the exact percentage changes each year with the school intake.

(7) All names in the Facebook project have been replaced by pseudonyms.

(8) http://www.eqao.com/Educators/educator.aspx?status=logout&Lang=E.

(9) Efforts are already being made to design such assessment tools – see Jamieson, 2005.

References

Bennett, S., Maton, K. and Kervin, L. (2008) The 'digital natives' debate: A critical review of the evidence. *British Journal of Educational Technology* 39 (5), 775–786.

Bezemer, J. and Kress, G. (2008) Writing in multimodal texts: A social semiotic account of designs for learning. *Written Communication* 25 (2), 166–195.

Bo-Kristensen, M. and Meyer, B. (2008) Transformations of the language laboratory. In T. Hansson (ed.) *Handbook of Research on Digital Information Technologies: Innovations, Methods, and Ethical Issues* (pp. 27–36). Hershey, PA: IGI Global.

Canagarajah, S. (2007) Lingua franca English, multilingual communities, and language acquisition. *The Modern Language Journal* 91 (4), 923–939.

Cope, B. and Kalantzis, M. (2009) A grammar of multimodality. *The International Journal of Learning* 16, 361–425, doi: 10.1080/15544800903076044.

Crystal, D. (2008) Texting. *ELT Journal* 16 (1), 77–83.

Dooley, K. (2008) Multiliteracies and pedagogy of new learning for students of English as an additional language. In A. Healey (ed.) *Multiliteracies and Expanding Landscapes: New Pedagogies for Student Diversity* (pp. 102–125). South Melbourne: Oxford University Press.

Education Quality and Accountability Office (EQAO) (2007) *Framework, Ontario Secondary Literacy Test* (rev. edn). Toronto, ON: EQAO. Online at http://www.ontla.on.ca/library/repository/mon/16000/270420.pdf.

Education Quality and Accountability Office (EQAO) (2009) *EQAO's Technical Report for the 2007–2008 Assessments.* Toronto: Queen's Printer for Ontario. Online at http://www.eqao.com/pdf_e/09/TechnicalReport_final_English.pdf.

Education Quality and Accountability Office (EQAO) (2010) *Grade 6 Assessment of Reading, Writing, Mathematics, Junior Division. Language: Student Booklet 1.* Toronto, ON: EQAO. Online at http://www.eqao.com/Parents/Elementary/036/BookletsandGuides.aspx?Lang=E&gr=036&yr=10.

Ellis, D. (2000) *The Breadwinner.* Toronto: Groundwood Books.

ETFO (2011) EQAO testing. The Elementary Teachers' Federation of Ontario. Online at http://www.etfo.ca/AdviceForMembers/PRSMattersBulletins/Pages/EQAO%20Testing.aspx.

ETS (2011) *Fast Facts.* Online at http://www.ets.org/about.

Freebody, P. and Lo Bianco, J. (1997) *Australian Literacies.* Canberra: Language Australia.

Freire, P. (2000) *Pedagogy of the Oppressed* (30th anniversary edn, M.B. Ramos, trans.). New York: Continuum (original work published 1970).

Gal, I. (2002) Adults' statistical literacy: Meanings, components, responsibilities. *International Statistical Review* 70 (1), 1–51.

Gee, J.P. (2010) *New Digital Media and Learning as an Emerging Area and 'Worked Examples' as One Way Forward.* Cambridge: The MIT Press.

Harklau, L., Losey, K.M. and Siegal, M. (1999) Linguistically diverse students and college writing: What is equitable and appropriate? In L. Harklau, K.M. Losey and M. Siegal (eds) *Generation 1.5 Meets College Composition: Issues in the Teaching of Writing to US-educated Learners of ESL* (pp. 1–16). Mahwah, NJ: Lawrence Erlbaum Associates.

Hurston, Z.N. (1937/1991) *Their Eyes Were Watching God.* Urbana: University of Illinois Press.

Jamieson, J. (2005) Trends in computer-based second language assessment. *Annual Review of Applied Linguistics* 25, 228–242.

Jenkins, H. (2006) *Convergence Culture: Where Old and New Media Collide.* New York: New York University Press.

Jenkins, H. (2009) *Confronting the Challenges of Participatory Culture: Media Education for the 21st Century.* Cambridge: The MIT Press.

Jewitt, C. (2002) The move from page to screen: The multimodal reshaping of school English. *Visual Communication* 1 (2), 171–195.

Kalantzis, M. and Cope, B. (2008) The assess-as-you-go writing assistant. Transforming student assessment. *New Learning: Transformational Designs for Pedagogy and Assessment.* Online at http://newlearningonline.com/news/assess-as-you-go/.

Kirsch, I.S., Jungeblut, A. and Mosenthal, P.B. (1998) The measurement of adult literacy. In S.T. Murray, I.S. Kirsch and L.B. Jenkins (eds) *Adult Literacy in OECD Countries: Technical Report on the First International Adult Literacy Survey* (pp. 105–134). Washington, DC: National Center for Education Statistics, US Department of Education.

Kress, G. (2009) What is a mode? In C. Jewitt (ed.) *The Routledge Handbook of Multimodal Analysis* (pp. 54–67). Abingdon: Routledge.

Lankshear, C. and Knobel, M. (2006) *New Literacies: Everyday Practices and Classroom Learning* (2nd edn). Berkshire: Open University Press.

Lotherington, H. (2009) Glocalization, representation and literacy education. *e-Learning* 6 (3), 274.

Lotherington, H. (2011) *Pedagogy of Multiliteracies: Rewriting Goldilocks.* New York: Routledge.

Lotherington, H. and Xu, Y. (2004) How to chat in English and Chinese: Emerging digital language conventions. *ReCALL* 16 (2), 308–329.

McLuhan, M. (1962) *Gutenberg Galaxy: The Making of Typographical Man.* Toronto: Toronto University Press.

Menken, K. (2008) *English Language Learners Left Behind: Standardized Testing as Language Policy.* Clevedon: Multilingual Matters.

Negroponte, N. (1995) *Being Digital.* New York: Knopf.

New London Group (1996) A pedagogy of multiliteracies: Designing social factors. *Harvard Educational Review* 66 (1), 60–92.

Nishimura, M.M. (2009) *The Medieval Imagination: Images in the Margins.* Los Angeles, CA: J. Paul Getty Museum.

Ontario Ministry of Education (2007) *The Ontario Curriculum, Grades 9 and 10: English.* Online at http://www.edu.gov.on.ca/eng/curriculum/secondary/english.html.

Radwan, N., Reckase, M.D. and Rogers, W.T. (2010) *Maintaining Comparability: The Move to a Single Literacy Score for the OSSLT.* Report prepared for the Education

Quality and Accountability Office (EQAO). Toronto: EQAO. Online at http://www.eqao.com/.

Sawyer, R.K. (2006) Education for innovation. *Thinking Skills and Creativity* 1, 41–48.

Sinclair, G. (2010) Exploring Canada's digital future. Featured 'big thinking' lecture at the Congress of the Humanities and Social Sciences, Concordia University, Montréal, Québec, May.

Spolsky, B. (1995) *Measured Words: The Development of Objective Language Testing.* Oxford: Oxford University Press.

Spolsky, B. (2008) Introduction. Language testing at 25: Maturity and responsibility? *Language Testing* 25 (3), 297–305.

Stoppard, T. (1967) *Rosencrantz and Guildenstern are Dead.* New York: Grove Press.

Tagliamonte, S. and Denis, D. (2008) LOL for real! Instant messaging and teen language. *American Speech* 83, 3–34.

Tan, J.P.-L. and McWilliam, E. (2009) From literacy to multiliteracies: Diverse learners and pedagogical practice. *Pedagogies: An International Journal* 4, 213–225. doi: 10.1080/15544800903076119.

Tan, L., Bopry, J. and Guo, L. (2010) Portraits of new literacies in two Singapore classrooms. *RELC Journal* 41, 5–17. doi: 10.1177/0033688210343864.

Thurlow, C. and Brown, A. (2003) Generation txt? The sociolinguistics of young people's text-messaging. *Discourse Analysis Online* 1 (1). Online at http://extra.shu.ac.uk/daol/articles/v1/n1/a3/thurlow2002003-paper.html.

Ware, P. and Warschauer, M. (2005) Hybrid literacy texts and practices in technology-intensive environments. *International Journal of Educational Research* 43, 432–445. doi: 10.1016/j.ijer.2006.07.008.

Watson, J. and Callingham, R. (2003) Statistical literacy: A complex hierarchical subject. *Statistics Education Research Journal* 2 (2), 3–46.

7 Beyond Labels and Categories in English Language Teaching: Critical Reflections on Popular Conceptualizations

Martin Dewey

Introduction

English Language Teaching (ELT) is unquestionably a global educational enterprise that operates on a vast scale. Particularly as practised in what might be described as the Western TESOL (Teaching English to Speakers of Other Languages) tradition, ELT is a huge multinational industry, employing vast numbers of language teachers and teacher trainers, and instructing ever growing numbers of language learners. This enterprise comprises a vast array of private language schools, university departments and colleges of further education offering English language tuition to non-mother tongue speakers; and all of which is overseen by numerous influential (sometimes powerful) stakeholders, including publishing houses, examination boards and professional organizations. In a growing number of educational contexts worldwide, English is being introduced into the curriculum as a compulsory subject (often from primary school age), or increasingly as a preferred medium for schooling, particularly in higher education.

The concept of English itself though, as both a subject and medium of education, is in need of considerable rethinking in light of the enormous contextual diversity surrounding the use of this language. In this chapter I therefore subject current professional practices in ELT to some 'reflective thought', which John Dewey (1933: 9) defined as 'active, persistent and careful consideration of any belief or supposed form of knowledge in the light of the grounds that support it'. In doing so, my purpose is to address the question 'what counts as English?', especially in relation to the extent to which English has become a globally diffuse language. To this end the following discussion calls into question the suitability of some conventional terms of reference, orienting most specifically to the following labels, EFL (English as a Foreign Language), ESL (English as a Second Language), the most widely used and accepted terms of demarcation of English used in the global ELT enterprise. The underlying premise of this critical reflection is that many of the terms of reference currently in favour are heavily laden with traditional intellectual assumptions about language that do not adequately reflect current realities regarding the global sociolinguistics of English. The discussion will therefore also consider the relatively new paradigm of ELF (English as a Lingua Franca), which marks a distinct attempt to rethink the way English is conceptualized.

Dominant Assumptions in ELT

The habitual and unmarked use of the conventional terms of reference mentioned above tends to give the impression that English is a stable and uniform phenomenon. However, as highlighted by recent debates in fields such as World Englishes and English as a Lingua Franca, English is not a unitary language neither in terms of its lexicogrammatical properties nor pragmatic conventions. There is a growing body of evidence that illustrates the extent to which local uses of English have given rise to widely varying norms and practices. A less monolithic, more heterogeneous view of English represents important challenges for educational institutions and practices, not least of which is the widely held assumption that Standard English (however we might define it) is the 'natural' goal of language learning worldwide.

English as a language name is both commercially marketable and conceptually problematic. When it is modified by adjunct phrases such as 'as second language' or 'as a foreign language', its meaning becomes even more complicated. Yet for the most part in language education, there has been little explicit focus on these many varied, often confusing, and seldom self-evident terms of reference. Working largely on unspoken assumptions, the concept of English itself tends not to be examined when reference is variously made to *English as an International Language, English as a World Language, English as a Global Language* and so on.[1] This has fuelled considerable debate recently within Applied Linguistics (see e.g. Seidlhofer & Berns, 2009). The casual way in which reference tends to be made to English does much to mask the complexities involved in the use of the language, particularly in contexts in which it operates as part of a multilingual environment. The aim here is to give a critical overview of some of this terminology, examining in the process the ideological and theoretical positions underlying each particular term.[2]

The dominant teaching methodology in ELT at present is usually referred to as the communicative approach, or CLT (Communicative Language Teaching). Although there is no single unifying framework of CLT, and although there have been various additions and recent reworkings of its methodological practices (see e.g. Harmer, 2007), there is a considerable sense of orthodoxy with regard to shared assumptions about language and communication. Similarly, although there have been recent challenges to the centralizing forces of this supposed orthodoxy (see e.g. Canagarajah, 1999; and see Kumaravadivelu, 2001, on the notion of post-method practices), it is still true to say that the approach continues to exert considerable influence worldwide. For this reason I give here some account of current theoretical and methodological tendencies in CLT, in order to help contextualize the subsequent arguments being put forward.

In their history of ELT, Howatt and Widdowson (2004: 326) describe the communicative approach as being characterized by 'the conviction that language teaching should take greater account of the way that language worked in the real world and try to be more responsive to the needs of learners in their efforts to acquire it'. There are two matters here that need to be given some critical reflection. First, if we do look in detail at the way language works we should begin to question some of the more conventional notions of what language is. To be properly concerned with the way language operates would involve adopting a more ethnographic approach to the collection and description of data. This is in line with the observation made by Leung (2005) that what is appropriate in language has to be determined empirically rather than be based on idealized and projected universalisms.

This entails a substantial shift in emphasis – one which turns the focus of attention to the occurrence of language in interactions, and which sees language as residing primarily in the co-constructed nature of discourse (see Leung & Street, Chapter 1, this volume). This in turn means that we need to look at language as a fundamentally social phenomenon. However, despite adoption of the term 'communicative competence' in ELT, in educational contexts language and communication have tended thus far to be conceptualized in a fairly restricted sense. The notion of communication is construed largely as the transition of information, and language is seen primarily as a set of grammar forms used formulaically in transactional exchanges, and usually modelled on a preferred variety of English.

Nevertheless, the CLT paradigm is generally characterized in ELT literature as a shift in focus away from the formal properties of language. The earlier centrality of grammatical structure came to be replaced by an emphasis on the way language functions communicatively. As the notion of communication gained momentum in early CLT, however, it increasingly tended to be interpreted in the curriculum as clearly definable functional objectives, such as 'accepting an invitation', 'making a complaint', and so on. From the early 1980s on the word 'communicative' came to be strongly associated with a notional-functional syllabus (see e.g. Munby, 1978). Undoubtedly, a good deal of day-to-day communication is composed of interactions in which speakers exchange information in order to achieve functions of this kind. But of course this is only part of what communication entails; during interaction of any kind there is a lot more happening than the transition of information. In even the most apparently 'functional' exchange, there is a complex interplay of personal and social beliefs, identities, relations and so on, all of which will shape the language being used (see Firth & Wagner, 1997).

As Widdowson (2004) remarks, the concept of communication in CLT has tended to be somewhat 'reductionist', with the design of courses often aimed simply at providing learners with formulae that could be used for rather 'a limited range of routine and rudimentary social purposes' (Widdowson, 2004: 356). This reductionism manifests itself in classrooms and teaching materials – at least early on – as a fairly narrow focus on the rehearsal of (often pre-scripted) routine dialogues in a limited number of formulaic social/institutional encounters, usually in service transactions involving customers, assistants, tourists, receptionists and so on. The nature of these dialogues may have changed considerably as a result of the insights gained from real-life examples, with the effect that the formal/textual properties being displayed in textbook materials are a much more accurate representation of how spoken interactions actually look, but in many cases the same relatively restricted repertoire of routines continues to predominate. The syllabus in many contemporary textbook materials in fact looks remarkably similar to the more overtly functional-notional syllabuses of two to three decades ago. A comparison of current popular materials (see e.g. Cunningham & Moor, 2005) with much earlier CLT resources (see e.g. Jones, 1981) shows that there is substantial similarity in terms of the presence and type of functional exponents included in the syllabus. In common with many published ELT resources, both these texts include a range of exponents for, among other functions, *asking for information, giving opinions, agreeing/ disagreeing, making comparisons* and so on.

Although the notional-functional syllabus has been largely superseded, the most current and widespread trend, Tasked Based Learning, which has replaced earlier interpretations of communicative methodology has arguably inherited the same reductive notion of communication (see Firth & Wagner, 1997, for a critical discussion). The critical issue here is that until recently CLT discourse has been almost exclusively concerned with discussion and development of approaches and methods, with the result that very little attention has been paid to addressing what exactly we mean when we talk about 'English' as a foreign/second/additional language. There have been numerous attempts to extol the virtues of the latest theories of learning and methodological practices, which has undoubtedly been important in the ongoing process of better understanding professional expertise in language teaching.

The usefulness of this quest for better and more effective pedagogy notwithstanding, what exactly does the 'E' represent in the many abbreviations and acronyms (EFL, ESL, ENL) currently being used during discussions of these theories and methods? Developments in the study of World Englishes and English as a Lingua Franca are two fields in particular which have made it necessary for ELT practitioners and stakeholders to give much more consideration to this issue. In light of this, I will now examine more closely what is meant and understood by these terms in ELT professional discourse.

English as a Foreign Language (EFL)

Traditionally, the teaching of English in contexts where it is not spoken as a first language by the majority population, and where it does not serve official intranational functions has been described as an English as a Foreign Language (EFL) setting. In addition, it is usually assumed that English is taught as a subject in schools, but in educational contexts where it is not normally the medium of instruction. Richards *et al.* (2002), in their professionally influential *Dictionary of English Language Teaching and Applied Linguistics*, also describe an EFL setting as one in which English is *not* 'a language of communication (e.g. in government, business, or industry) within the country' (2002: 124). In this definition communication is equated with the business of government, commerce and industry. This is quite an arresting claim to make. It may on the surface seem fairly unproblematic to observe that in an EFL country there is no use of English outside classroom settings, that the language is thought to occur almost exclusively in formal language learning contexts. However, this claim no longer fully reflects the current reality.

As Jenkins (2009) observes, in countries traditionally defined as EFL, the language is increasingly being adopted for intranational purposes, especially in institutional settings such as higher education. In the specific context of China, Nunan (2003) comments on how political and economic reform has led to the introduction of English-medium teaching in many universities, which is now a requirement in certain subject areas, including information technology, economics and law (for a related discussion see Kirkpatrick, 2007). New developments of this kind are easily overlooked if we continue to classify China and other 'expanding circle' (Kachru, 1992) contexts as simply EFL settings. The term nevertheless continues to be dominant.

Until relatively recently, EFL was the most widely used term in the ELT profession, and certainly the one most closely associated with the development of communicative methodologies. Indeed, the term leant itself to the naming of the teaching awards developed by UCLES (University of Cambridge Local Examination Syndicate), which were at the time CTEFLA (Certificate in Teaching English as a Foreign Language to Adults) and DTEFLA (Diploma in Teaching English as a Foreign Language to Adults). It has also been adopted by many professional organizations, including IATEFL (International Association for Teachers of English as a Foreign Language), with 'TEFL' being used outside the profession to refer to the profession itself.

There are many grounds on which we might want to object to this term, however, especially with regard to the connotations of *foreign*. The word has strong associations with concepts such as 'coming from outside', 'being alien', 'unfamiliar', 'strange', and with additional associations of 'not belonging' or 'being unwelcome'. Secondary meanings include 'being uncharacteristic', as in the following example given in the *Encarta World English Dictionary*, 'Such outbursts are quite foreign to her.' This is problematic on several levels. Given its much trumpeted status as a world language, especially the many arguments being put forward about the detachment of English from its native-speaker contexts (see below for further elaboration), it is difficult to sustain the notion of English as 'foreign'. If we take account of the associated meanings described above, then by describing English as a foreign language, the question is 'outside of where?'/'not belonging where?'.

As has by now long been argued (most directly with regard to ELT by Widdowson, 1994), widespread internationalization means that English has long ceased to be the preserve of its traditional native-speakers. In other words, ownership of the language no longer resides exclusively with speakers from the conventional English as a Native Language (ENL) countries. It is appropriated and manipulated to suit the specific purposes of contexts in which it is spoken, often far removed from its original surroundings. As English has travelled, it has not remained intact but has diversified, with new linguacultural ties being created through processes of nativization. In a growing number of contexts around the world, English has become part of the fabric of local communication.

This is especially the case in India, for instance, where English has the status of 'associate official' language (also see next section), and where, in the words of Jenkins (2009: 46), English 'has become bound up with Indian national consciousness and identity'. Gargesh (2008: 231) describes English in India as 'the most potent medium of higher education, perhaps the sole medium of science and technology', adding that '[m]ost books, newspapers reports, seminars and so forth directed to a nationwide audience are brought out in this language'. It is the official and institutional status of the language that leads to local appropriation and indigenization. In many other contexts, especially in a growing number of European countries (particularly in Scandinavia), English has no official status as such but it is also increasingly performing important intranational functions, especially as a medium of instruction in higher education (see e.g. Breiteneder, 2009). In other words, English can belong to whoever chooses to make it their own through communicating and interacting in the language. It is 'at home', so to speak, wherever it is spoken, and in that sense it is problematic to describe English as foreign. What this requires at the conceptual level is that we untie our notion of English from any attachment to a single ancestry, and that we instead pluralize our conceptualization of notions such as 'heritage' and 'belonging' in relation to this language.

In addition, part of the problem with EFL labelling is that our understanding of the concept of foreignness is largely dependent on the concept of nationhood. When we describe something as foreign we usually understand this to mean that it originates from another country. Again, this is clearly evident in the way the word is defined, such as in the following, 'located in or coming from another country' (*Collins English Dictionary*: 604). The connection between language and the nation state, although historically a relatively recent idea, exerts a powerful influence on the way in which we perceive language. Despite the transformative impact of globalization (see e.g. arguments presented in Rosenau, 1997; and Dewey, 2007, for a discussion of these in relation to English), which has seen reductions in the influence of the nation state, in terms of our understanding of what a language is the nation continues to be of central importance. This is perhaps unsurprising given the role language has played in the rise of nationhood, both during the 19th century in Europe, and then again in the mid-20th century as new nation states emerged during the era of post-colonialism.

With the emergence of a single dominant language (often the case in Europe, such as 'Italian', essentially a Tuscan dialect, becoming the language of Italy), thus playing a unifying role in the emergence of a national consciousness (see especially Gambarota, 2011, on this), and more planned selection of a single code in multilingual states (such as the selection of Malay as the official language in Malaysia), the notion of a national language has had huge symbolic power. The idea of one language for one nation is thus a persistent one. Although the physicalities of language and nation in fact seldom coincide, the assumed link between them remains prominent. In language planning and policy the identification of a single national language is very strongly associated with a sense of national identity and political unity.[3]

In this way of thinking we tend to see language as an entity and as a fixed set of means of communication, a bounded phenomenon that can be (quite literally) counted and thus pluralized. This has led to the possibility of describing language as national varieties, such as in the distinction made between American and British English, but also in the description of Englishes such as Indian English and Singaporean English. Yet, there is a very real sense in which language is not an entity, but is rather a more fluid, dynamic phenomenon. Research in World Englishes, for instance, has revealed the large extent to which language resources, often from many varied linguacultural sources, tend to become blended together in the formation of local Englishes (see e.g. Kirkpatrick, 2010, for a recent overview). In the context of Southeast Asia, this is particularly noteworthy. Tan (2009), for example, shows how Malaysian English has been shaped by lexical borrowing from an exceptionally rich language mix, citing, among others: numerous Chinese languages, Hokkien, Hakka, Cantonese; languages spoken by the Indian community, Tamil, Telegu, Singhalese, Urdu, Bengali; various languages indigenous to the Malaysian peninsular and Borneo; as well as several Malay dialects.

By referring to contexts in which English is not traditionally the mother tongue with the term EFL, we are thus ignoring this dynamism and masking the exceptional linguistic diversity it gives rise to. In short, it is an outmoded perception of what English is in sociolinguistic reality. To see English as a 'foreign' language is to overstate the link between the language and a single nation – obviously English is no longer simply the language of England (or even of Britain, the UK, or indeed any of the other anglophone nations). We may well wish to continue to make territorial claims about the language, but to refer to English as 'foreign' quite simply fails to recognize that the language has already been appropriated, re-territorialized, and in the process re-nativized in so many contexts far removed from its supposed 'original' national base(s).

English as a Second Language (ESL)

By contrast with EFL, the description of English as a Second Language (ESL) has two distinct uses. First, it is often used in ELT to describe the learning and teaching of English to resident learners in ENL contexts, a matter discussed further at the end of this section. Second, it can also refer to the presence of English in countries where the language usually has some form of official status, but where it is generally not spoken as a first language, at least not by the majority population. In these settings, such as in the case of India, Singapore and Nigeria, English tends to serve largely as a means of communication at an institutional level, in say government, law and higher education. Studying the development of English in these contexts has now become established as a major discipline, *World Englishes* (see e.g. Kachru *et al.*, 2006), where the pluralization of 'English' serves to indicate the extent to which the language has diversified as a result of its appropriation and relocalization. As a field of enquiry then World Englishes is concerned with the description and analysis of *nativized* varieties, also variously described as 'New Englishes', 'indigenized varieties', 'institutionalized varieties', as well as 'Postcolonial Englishes' (Schneider, 2007), a term which specifically highlights the historical connection of English in these settings with British and American colonialism.

A primary aim of work in this field has been to investigate the distinctive nature of particular 'outer circle' Englishes for the legitimization of these as varieties in their own right. In this respect, it has now been convincingly demonstrated that speech patterns serve as markers of identity and group membership just as much in say India or Singapore as in the UK or the US. Nativized Englishes may share some aspects of a common colonial history, but it is also true to say that they all display very distinctive characteristics, each with their own indicative patterns of discourse, lexis, grammar and phonology. If we take a closer look at any of these manifestations of the language, each variety demonstrates the extent to which English has diverged away from how it was spoken when it was first introduced (or generally imposed) in these settings. Lim (2007), for example, provides a comprehensive account of a very distinctive feature of English in Singapore, the widespread use of discourse particles (also often referred to as pragmatic particles) such as *lah, ah, hah, what, lor, hor, nah leh, ma, meh* and so on. Lim details the forms and functions of these particles, establishing in the process the origins and evolution of these highly characteristic features in the development of colloquial Singapore English.

In the latter half of the 20th century, as political independence was increasingly fought for and won throughout Africa and Asia, English tended to be retained in order that it should serve as a relatively 'neutral' lingua franca in often complex multilingual settings. This is especially the case in contexts where the selection of an indigenous language could have led to political tension, thus threatening the often fragile unity of newly established sovereign states. There can be no such thing as complete neutrality of course, but if a European language (particularly one with an imperial legacy) is to function more or less neutrally, it needs to become decolonized. In other words, English must be substantially refashioned, not only to suit the immediate purposes of the local setting, but also to enable disassociation of the language with its colonial past. It is essential therefore that the nativization of these Englishes is systematically documented, and the validity of their identities as distinct varieties is promoted. This is exactly what the World Englishes scholars have gone a long way in achieving (and despite continued resistance to the legitimization of indigenized varieties) (see e.g. Schneider, 2007, on the importance of acceptance in the evolutionary cycle of new Englishes). Given the value and importance of work of this kind, it is wholly questionable whether we can continue to describe English in these contexts as a 'second' language. The usual assumption is that if someone speaks a second language, then they are a non-native-speaker of that language. But surely, if we refer to English as being nativized, then this assumption is no longer sustainable. (In light of this argument Dewey & Jenkins, 2010, refer to both inner circle and outer circle Englishes as native varieties.)[4]

In addition, as with the arguments presented in relation to the term EFL, the pace of demographic and social change brought about by globalization means that we need to rethink the way we see English in these settings. A growing number of English users in post-colonial settings speak it as a primary language, where it is spoken at home and not exclusively for institutional purposes (or as Jenkins, 2009, points out, even in some instances as their only language). A further problem lies in the monolingual bias underlying the terms 'first' and 'second' language. In most contexts conventionally categorized as ESL, English functions as one language among many – for most speakers it operates as part of a complex multilingual repertoire. As we have seen, this is especially the case say in contexts such as Malaysia (see e.g. Tan, 2009) or Singapore (see e.g. Lim, 2007). For this reason, languages cannot simply be separated one from the other in such a way that allows a numerical value to be assigned to them.

Another use of the term ESL is made in reference to the teaching and learning of English to immigrant populations in countries traditionally defined as English-speaking. In the UK, the acronym ESOL (English for Speakers of Other Languages) has become very firmly established as the preferred term, largely replacing this additional use of ESL, especially in contexts of adult education. In mainstream schooling in the UK the term EAL (English as an Additional Language) is primarily used to refer to children in the school system who do not speak English as a mother tongue. As a result of rapid growth in population movements, brought about by the intensifying globalization of trade and resulting increases in flows of cross-border economic migration, the notion of a 'second' language has increasingly to be conceptualized in relation to linguistic minorities in conventionally English dominant countries. The consequences that these developments give rise to are, though, far from straightforward. As has already been discussed, language issues are tied to much wider social and political developments. In the case of the conventional English-speaking countries, traditionally seen as predominantly monolingual contexts, especially (though not exclusively) the urban/metropolitan areas are becoming ever more multilingual in make-up (see e.g. Block, 2006), all of which necessitates a substantial rethinking of the customary naming practices of English language varieties.

English as a Lingua Franca (ELF)

In the past decade or so, and with growing momentum especially in the past few years, the term ELF has emerged to describe the use of English in settings where it functions as a contact language among speakers of different linguacultural backgrounds.

Ever since the publication of a seminal paper, Seidlhofer (2001), in which persuasive arguments were put forward in calling for the systematic study of English in lingua franca settings, ELF has emerged as a distinct research paradigm. Empirical investigation into lingua franca English shares some important common ground with World Englishes, in that partly the focus has been on the identification of core linguistic features. This, for example, was an essential undertaking in the pioneering work carried out in this field, in which Jenkins (2000) provides an account of the phonological features required to maintain intelligibility in lingua franca communication. There are though some essential differences between ELF and World Englishes at the conceptual level.

A critical point is that ELF interactions most typically occur in highly variable socio/linguacultural networks, as opposed to more clearly definable communities. The globalization of communicative events through digital technologies means that these networks can be especially transient in nature. The contexts in which English is spoken, therefore, do not always fit very easily into the customary categories of analysis as inherited from early work in sociolinguistics. This requires considerable reorientation in our thinking about the relationship between language and social practices – a thorough discussion of which is presented in Heller (2008), in which she illustrates recent ideological shifts in sociolinguistic theory and practice. Of particular relevance here is her account of the limitations of attempting to apply conventionally fixed notions of phenomena such as social position, linguistic form and community boundaries. This has strong resonance with some of the arguments put forward in discussions of the nature of ELF (see especially Seidlhofer, 2006; Dewey, 2009).

While World Englishes is concerned with the use of English in outer circle settings, it is essential to note that the focus of ELF research is not simply the use of English in the expanding circle. In other words, World Englishes research locates English geographically, whereas ELF research has largely sought to untie linguistic description from conventional notions of distinct groups of speakers (customarily determined by class, gender, geographic location and so on). There have already been several notable attempts in the literature to rethink notions such as 'community' and 'variety', and other conventional categories of analysis in sociolinguistic work. In particular, Seidlhofer (2006) calls into question a number of existing conceptual frameworks, which in her view need updating in light of recent socio-political developments. Our understanding of community, for example, has radically shifted in the past decade or so. The concept now has far less to do with proximity, geographic location or group cohesion, and far more to do with a more virtual notion of interactional networks that may operate entirely independently of physical setting.

In relation to language in education, the key arguments put forward by researchers in ELF, as well as by others participating in the debate about the global scope of English, represent an important challenge to widely held assumptions about language learning goals. The significance of applying this label as an alternative to describing English as 'foreign' language is explicitly addressed by Jenkins (2000: 11) in her following appraisal of the term.

> This term would have a number of immediate advantages: ELF emphasizes the role of English in communication between speakers from different L1s, i.e. the primary reason for learning English today; it suggests the idea of community as opposed to alienness; it emphasizes that people have something in common rather than their differences; it implies that 'mixing' languages is acceptable [... and ...] finally, the Latin name symbolically removes the ownership of English from the Anglos both to no one and, in effect, to everyone.

Jenkins goes on to suggest that 'it remains to be seen whether ELF ultimately catches on' (2000: 11). The term has most definitely caught on. It has emerged in recent years as the preferred term among researchers working in the field to the extent that ELF has been founded as a new empirical and theoretical paradigm, with the first international conference devoted to the subject (Helsinki, 2008) having now become established as an annual event, with the University of Southampton hosting the second (2009), with subsequent conferences scheduled in Vienna (2010) and Hong Kong (2011). The themes currently of central concern include the sociolinguistics of ELF, its descriptive methodology, and the implications of ELF on language policy and language education.

In the case of language education, research in this area has now gradually begun to have an impact on current practice, at least at a policy level. In September 2008, Cambridge ESOL, the main providers of teaching awards for English language teachers in the UK, completely overhauled the existing DELTA (Diploma in English Language Teaching to Adults) scheme by introducing a new modular-based syllabus. Among the many additions made to the substantially reviewed curriculum content was inclusion of World Englishes, Global English and English as a Lingua Franca as topics about which teachers are expected to develop an understanding. It remains to be seen what direct impact these changes will have on classroom practice, a matter that will require considerable empirical attention (see e.g. Dewey, 2011). It is clear though that the principal tenets of an ELF perspective on language in education have started to enter public discourse in ELT methodology, as well no doubt as the individual consciousness of practicing language teachers and teacher educators.

Modelling English

There has been much debate in the past decade or so about the ongoing internationalization of the English language, with considerable empirical and theoretical investigation into the characteristics, status, attitudes towards, and pedagogical implications of the enormous diversity of English in the world.

What research in these fields has very clearly demonstrated is that English cannot be thought of as a unitary form. We may have become accustomed to referring to languages as if they were unified bounded phenomena, perhaps partly for convenience sake but also undoubtedly for ideological reasons (a matter taken up further below), but any close examination of language in use reveals the complexities involved in interaction. This of course makes the labelling and modelling of language in any situation a highly problematic affair. Given that English is so globally widespread, and there is so much political, financial, emotional investment in its teaching and learning, the situation becomes even more important to address.

Developments in World Englishes and ELF thus clearly have major implications for language learning and teaching, and do so on several levels. Canagarajah (2005), talking from a perspective of critical pedagogy, argues that it is essential for the teaching profession to fully consider the importance of the concept of World Englishes to current pedagogic practices. He extols the virtue of teachers adopting a more 'levelled' as opposed to 'hierarchical' approach. This would involve decentring both the language model itself and the teaching methodologies used to present it.

Beyond CLT and Language as a Bounded Phenomenon

Canagarajah (2005) proposes the adoption of a multi-norm approach to English, where norms and standards that are found outside ENL contexts are applied whenever relevant. He suggests that a disciplinary shift is in fact already in progress, one which entails a move towards a system of linguistic plurality where knowledge is locally defined and information flows are multilateral. In this revised framework, traditional terminology, such as 'native', 'established' and 'authenticity', are replaced respectively by 'expert', 'local' and 'relevance' (see Leung *et al.*, 1997; Rampton, 1990). This effectively disentangles the discussion of pedagogic models from the native/non-native distinction. It also means methods can be determined as relevant to a particular context, making it more possible for learners and teachers to consider alternatives to an ENL model. The notion of 'repertoire' therefore becomes more important than 'target language', where correctness gives way to negotiation, and mastery of grammatical rules is superseded by 'metalinguistic awareness' (Canagarajah, 2005: xxv).

Effective communication is more than adherence to native-speaker norms or the mastery of a predetermined grammar. It has much more to do with awareness of linguistic and cultural difference, and ability to accommodate towards an interlocutor (also see Leung & Street, Chapter 1, this volume). Recent research in ELF, for example, has been undertaken from the premise that what is appropriate and effective in language use is wholly context sensitive. Findings in this field have begun to show how flexibility in the use of linguistic resources can enhance effectiveness and efficiency of communication (see Cogo & Dewey, 2006). In other words, being adaptive is an important part of the interactional skills of accomplished communicators, especially in language contact or lingua franca situations. The challenge then for conceptualizing language in education is how to untie notions of competence from association with a definitive set of codified language forms.

Throughout the history of modern ELT though it has been assumed, regardless of social setting, that the model of language to be introduced in the classroom should be based on the norms of 'Standard English'. This may seem a pretty straightforward and uncontroversial idea. But this is a term that is in fact highly problematic, not least of all because of the difficulty involved in trying to define it. Howatt and Widdowson (2004: 320), for example, refer to classroom models as being based on 'the standard English used by educated people in all English-speaking countries'.

What is apparent in definitions of this kind is the extent to which the complex nature of language is being glossed over. Howatt and Widdowson, for instance, make no distinction between written and spoken usage, nor do they consider where language is written or spoken, between what users and for what purpose. In addition to these issues, there are by now multiple Standard Englishes, and the key question that must be asked in the context of the above debate is 'what exactly counts as an English-speaking country?' Careful thought needs to be given to what criteria we use to determine whether or not a context should be categorized as English-speaking. We also need then to be very mindful of who we describe as an English speaker, and must be prepared to go beyond the conventional, narrow definition of this term.

For many speakers of English, the language is simply one of many languages available to them. The issue is further complicated as a result of language shift: because in many multilingual settings the first language(s) an individual learns may not always continue to be dominant in all domains, referring to a speaker's use of English as either a 'first' or 'second' language may do very little to indicate the extent of a speaker's competence in or identification with that language. The assumption that we can easily assign a number to a language is largely dependent on the notion that monolingualism is the norm, and that multilingualism is the co-presence of more than one monolingual repertoire within an individual; in other words, it depends on a rather fanciful idea that we can straightforwardly ascertain which single code is the appropriate one for a given context. In short, designating speakers of English as either 'first' or 'second' language users and then recommending a single pedagogic model on the basis of this only serves to mask the sociolinguistic complexity of multilingual societies.

Multilingualism has tended not to be incorporated in the theoretical and methodological discourses of ELT. Standardized (i.e. monolingual) norms, especially as defined in relation to the notion of a national variety (American English or British English) have acted as a kind of restraining force on the language, serving as the mechanism by which the linguistic innovations of certain users – primarily 'educated' speakers of ENL varieties – are sanctioned, while the innovations of all other users are classified as 'deviations'. As a result, ELT has tended to regard as self-evident that the objectives of language learning are necessarily defined according to approximation towards an idealized set of target norms. This can be seen as part of a broad tradition for regarding language as an 'object' of enquiry, an autonomous and reified system, understood as an entity that is largely external to its speakers. As Holborow (1999) observes, the structuralist legacy of studying language as an abstract, socially disconnected system continues to influence our thinking, with the result that language systems are seen as primary, while the role of language users is reduced simply to conforming to the rules. In education, this reification of the system is deep rooted and pervasive, with language most often defined and related to in terms of established rules of usage (see Dewey, 2009, for a more thorough discussion).

In the conventional approach to language adopted in ELT, despite moves to adopt a more communicative methodology, there has been a heavy bias towards grammatical competence. An individual's full range of verbal abilities is not well accounted for since competence is largely understood and assessed in relation to adherence to a finite set of language forms. Leung (2005) explains how communicative competence, a concept originally developed for ethnographic research, has tended to be interpreted in ELT in a very narrow sense, with the transfer of the concept from research to pedagogy bringing with it over abstraction and idealization.

This results in a culture of thinking about language and communication in which language is 'fixed' as a set of norms. Grammar is thus seen as a precondition for communication, and intelligibility is regarded as norm dependent. For the most part ELT remains very attached to the idea that there is a single 'correct' standard usage, characterized by the selection of norms as a means of eradicating language differences, which tend to be seen as a threat to intelligibility. This attachment to normativity does not fit very well with the communicative realities of English speakers, however. For many speakers, an interactional setting may require numerous combinations and admixtures of languages, with hybrid selections of language resources being constructed from within a very varied repertoire. This has major consequences for the way we conceptualize language in all educational contexts. It has particular resonance when we consider, for instance, the role of English in international schools and the growing complexity of these educational settings (see e.g. Hayden *et al.*, 2007), where all manner of English varieties and languages are in regular and sustained contact with each other.

Conventional assumptions about the supposed paramountcy of ENL thus need to be rethought. Research in ELF holds major implications for English language professionals and, in particular, we need to reconsider the extent to which it is viable for ELT practitioners to continue to administer external norms (see also Jenkins, 2006, on these matters). Key to this is an understanding of the inherent variability and adaptability of human languages, and the ultimate heterogeneous nature of any linguistic system. This represents a substantial challenge to orthodox opinion in CLT. An important educational move is to raise awareness amongst teachers of English of this fluidity, and of the complex relationship between abstracted language models and the variable nature of communication. Recognition of the pluralistic nature of language, therefore, brings with it a substantial need to reconsider key beliefs and practices in language education.

Conclusions

Given the above arguments, the designation of speakers of English as either ENL, ESL, EFL and so on is wholly problematic. Attempting to model the spread of English globally by placing it inside categories in this way means we are ultimately trying to contain what is a very fluid phenomenon (see Jenkins, 2009, for a critical overview of the various attempts there have been for classifying types of English worldwide). There is ultimately, therefore, tension between the variable actuality of language in use and the need to select a model for classroom teaching and language assessment. It is important in language education that the level of abstraction required to model English is made explicit.

Whichever of these labels is seen in whatever context to be the most appropriate, there are some very profound considerations to be taken into account. The various debates about the global presence of English lead not simply to a rethinking of the current trends in the naming of types of English. These discourses also represent a challenge to the very nature of conceptual beliefs about what language itself is. As we have seen, the culture of language in ELT is primarily characterized by a limited view that English is made up of largely static systems of lexis, phonology and grammar. In terms of pedagogic resources, this notion of language tends to materialize in the form of pre-fabricated, formulaic expressions, especially those that are most often used for transactional purposes.

There has though already been some movement in significantly new directions. Ferguson's (2006) discussion of language policy and planning in education provides an overview of the implications of recent research to the selection of models for language teaching. Seidlhofer *et al.* (2006) observe that raising awareness of how different languages operate in communities has in some contexts begun to be put into practice. In particular, there is much to be gained regarding perceptions of language varieties if learners and teachers develop better understanding of multilingualism and the multifaceted nature of most speech communities.

What the proliferation of terms used to describe English indicates most clearly is that the English language is especially diverse. In all its various guises around the world – along with any professional activity directly associated with it, and most especially ELT – English is going through a substantial period of transition. For this reason it is inevitable that we should find ourselves confronted with a wide range of choices in the terms that we use. There is still as yet a good deal that is unsettled with regard not only to the level of acceptance given to each of these terms, or the extent of agreement surrounding their contextual suitability, but also in fact over the precise meaning of a term itself. This reflexive examination of the labels in ELT suggests that it would be a good idea to explicate and critically evaluate the assumptions and values associated with the established terms of reference, and to seek out alternatives wherever appropriate.

Notes

(1) There are many terms currently in circulation that describe the phenomenon of English internationally. Among those not directly addressed in this article, the most commonplace are probably EIL (English as an International Language), World English and Global English. Each of these terms tends also to imply that the use of English internationally entails a universal form – yet in actual fact there is no such thing as a single international variety of the language. English as a language name is an abstract and somewhat vague notion. For this reason the preferred terms used to describe this phenomenon here are World Englishes, because of its inherent pluralization, and English as a Lingua Franca, because work in this field has explicitly set out to investigate the diverse nature of English.

(2) There have been several recent attempts to identify key differences between the main terms of reference in current use, the most thorough of which is probably Jenkins' (2006) discussion of the implications of research into World Englishes and English as a Lingua Franca for ELT. Jenkins provides several important points of clarification with regard to the principal terms of reference in light of the conceptual complexification that acknowledgement of the diversity of this language entails.

(3) In recent years there have been several concerted efforts to reassert the status of supposed national languages, especially where these are thought to serve a unifying role. In the United States of America, for example, the English Only Movement has

sought to push for legislation that would grant official status to English as the language of the USA. Campaigns and movements of this kind continue to emerge, especially as a response to the perceived threat that growing multilingualism brings with it.

(4) There have been lengthy critical discussions of the notion of nativeness in language learning and teaching (see e.g. Parakrama, 1995; Rampton, 1990).

References

Block, D. (2006) *Multilingual Identities in a Global City: London Stories.* Houndmills, Basingstoke: Palgrave Macmillan.

Breiteneder, A. (2009) English as a lingua franca in Europe: An empirical perspective. *World Englishes* 28 (2), 256–269.

Canagarajah, A.S. (1999) *Resisting Linguistic Imperialism in English Teaching.* Oxford: Oxford University Press.

Canagarajah, A.S. (2005) Introduction. In A.S. Canagarajah (ed.) *Reclaiming the Local in Language Policy and Practice* (pp. xiii–xxx). Mahwah, NJ: Lawrence Earlbaum Associates.

Cogo, A. and Dewey, M. (2006) Efficiency in ELF communication: From pragmatic motives to lexicogrammatical innovation. *Nordic Journal of English Studies* 5 (2), 59–94.

Collins English Dictionary (2003) 6th edn. Glasgow: HarperCollins.

Cunningham, S. and Moor, P. (2005) *New Cutting Edge: Intermediate Students' Book.* Harlow: Longman ELT.

Dewey, J. (1933) *How We Think.* New York: D.C. Heath & Co.

Dewey, M. (2007) English as a lingua franca and globalization: An interconnected perspective. *International Journal of Applied Linguistics* 17 (3), 332–354.

Dewey, M. (2009) English as a lingua franca: Heightened variability and theoretical implications. In A. Mauranen and E. Ranta (eds) *English as a Lingua Franca: Studies and Findings* (pp. 60–83). Newcastle: Cambridge Scholars Press.

Dewey, M. (2011) Accommodative ELF talk and teacher knowledge. In A. Archibald, A. Cogo and J. Jenkins (eds) *Latest Trends in ELF Research* (pp. 205–228). Newcastle: Cambridge Scholars Press.

Dewey, M. and Jenkins, J. (2010) English as a lingua franca in the global context: Interconnectedness, variation, and change. In T. Omoniyi and M. Saxena (eds) *Contending with Globalization in World Englishes* (pp. 72–92). Bristol: Multilingual Matters.

Ferguson, G. (2006) *Language Planning and Education.* Edinburgh: Edinburgh University Press.

Firth, A. and Wagner, J. (1997) On discourse, communication, and (some) fundamental concepts in SLA research. *The Modern Language Journal* 81, 285–300.

Gambarota, P. (2011) *Irresistible Signs: The Genius of Language and Italian National Identity.* Toronto: University of Toronto Press.

Gargesh, R. (2008) Indian English: Phonology. In R. Mesthrie (ed.) *Varieties of English Vol 4: Africa, South and Southeast Asia* (pp. 231–243). Berlin: Mouton de Gruyter.

Harmer, J. (2007) *The Practice of English Language Teaching* (4th edn). Harlow: Longman.

Hayden, M., Thompson, J. and Levy, J. (eds) (2007) *The Sage Handbook of Research in International Education.* London: Sage.

Heller, M. (2008) Language and the nation-state: Challenges to socio-linguistic theory. *Journal of Socio-linguistics* 12 (4), 504–524.

Holborow, M. (1999) *The Politics of English: A Marxist View of Language*. London: Sage.

Howatt, A.P.R. and Widdowson, H.G. (2004) *A History of English Language Teaching* (2nd edn). Oxford: Oxford University Press.

Jenkins, J. (2000) *The Phonology of English as an International Language*. Oxford: Oxford University Press.

Jenkins, J. (2006) Current perspectives on teaching World Englishes and English as a lingua franca. *TESOL Quarterly* 40 (1), 157–181.

Jenkins, J. (2009) *World Englishes: A Resource Book for Students* (2nd edn). London: Routledge.

Jones, L. (1981) *Functions of English Student's Book: Course for Upper-intermediate and More Advanced Students*. Cambridge: Cambridge University Press.

Kachru, B. (ed.) (1992) *The Other Tongue: English across Cultures* (2nd edn). Urbana: University of Illinois Press.

Kachru, B., Kachru, Y. and Nelson, C. (2006) *The Handbook of World Englishes*. Oxford: Blackwells.

Kirkpatrick, A. (2007) *World Englishes: Implications for International Communication and English Language Teaching*. Cambridge: Cambridge University Press.

Kirkpatrick, A. (2010) *English as a Lingua Franca in ASEAN*. Hong Kong: Hong Kong University Press.

Kumaravadivelu, B. (2001) Toward a postmethod pedagogy. *TESOL Quarterly* 35 (4), 537–560.

Leung, C. (2005) Convivial communication: Recontextualizing communicative competence. *International Journal of Applied Linguistics* 15 (2), 119–144.

Leung, C., Harris, R. and Rampton, B. (1997) The idealised native speaker, reified ethnicities, and classroom realities. *TESOL Quarterly* 31 (3), 543–560.

Lim, L. (2007) Mergers and acquisitions: On the ages and origins of Singapore English particles. *World Englishes* 26 (4), 446–473.

Munby, J. (1978) *Communicative Syllabus Design*. Cambridge: Cambridge University Press.

Nunan, D. (2003) The impact of English as a global language on educational policies and practices in the Asia-Pacific region. *TESOL Quarterly* 37 (4), 589–613.

Parakrama, A. (1995) *De-hegemonizing Language Standards: Learning from (Post)colonial Englishes about 'English'*. Basingstoke: Macmillan Press.

Rampton, B. (1990) Displacing the 'native speaker': Expertise, affiliation and inheritance. *ELT Journal* 44 (2), 97–101.

Richards, J., Platt, J. and Platt, H. (2002) *Longman Dictionary of Language Teaching and Applied Linguistics* (2nd edn). Harlow: Longman.

Rosenau, J. (1997) *Along the Domestic-foreign Frontier*. Cambridge: Cambridge University Press.

Schneider, E. (2007) *Postcolonial English: Varieties Around the World*. Cambridge: Cambridge University Press.

Seidlhofer, B. (2001) Closing a conceptual gap: The case for a description of English as a lingua franca. *International Journal of Applied Linguistics* 15 (2), 326–345.

Seidlhofer, B. (2006) English as a lingua franca and communities of practice. In S. Volk-Birke and J. Lippert (eds) *Anglistentag 2006 Halle Proceedings* (pp. 307–318). Trier: Wissenschaftlicher Verlag Trier.

Seidlhofer, B. and Berns, M. (2009) Perspectives on English as a lingua franca: Introduction. *World Englishes* 28 (2), 190–191.

Seidlhofer, B., Breiteneder, A. and Pitzl, M-L. (2006) English as a lingua franca in Europe: Challenges for applied linguistics. *Annual Review of Applied Linguistics* 26, 3–34.

Soukhanov, A.H. (1999) *Encarta World English Dictionary*. New York: St Martin's Press.

Tan, S.I. (2009) Lexical borrowing from Chinese languages in Malaysian English. *World Englishes* 28 (4), 451–484.

Widdowson, H.G. (1994) The ownership of English. *TESOL Quarterly* 28 (2), 377–389.

Widdowson, H.G. (2004) A perspective on recent trends. In A.P.R. Howatt and H.G. Widdowson (eds) *A History of English Language Teaching* (2nd edn) (pp. 353–372). Oxford: Oxford University Press.

Concluding Remarks

Constant Leung and Brian Street

In the opening chapter of the volume we suggest that two major changes are necessary in the approaches to the medium of English: (a) the notion of communicative competence in English, hitherto largely referenced to metropolitan native-speaker norms, has to be expanded to take account of the multi-faceted uses that can be observed in different world locations and for a variety of purposes, and (b) the popular belief that literacy is simply a technical 'skill' which confers universal benefits should be replaced with a social practice view that recognises situated variations and diversity. Collectively, the chapters in this volume address these issues and, we believe, make a strong case for such changes. In Chapter 1 we set out the main theoretical issues such changes raise, notably with respect to the uses made of Hymes' notion of communicative competence in addressing contemporary language learning and the extension of understanding literacy towards social practices and multiple literacies, whilst Dewy picks up many of the conceptual problems reflected in the language labels widely used in ELT and language education more generally from a critical perspective. The other authors draw upon research experience in a range of countries: South Africa, Australia, the USA, Hong Kong, Canada and the UK to reinforce these points, some addressing language policy directly (Lin, Prinsloo, Snyder & Beale), whilst others focus on language and literacy in relation to such policy and practice (Horner & Lu, Lotherington & Ronda). We see such work as helping to map out future directions in the field that may draw upon a wider range of countries and contexts; it also, we believe, provides a strong foundation for further extension of both the theories and their applications. As English becomes even more generally available for communicative use and widely adopted as a medium for education, in multiple and changing contexts, so the shifts we have witnessed to date will entail further development – in terms, for instance, of what counts as a 'medium' in such contexts; and in terms of how spoken English relates to the range of written media available through both print and internet, and the range of modes, evident in the increased mixing and meshing of spoken, written and visual.

This volume, then, represents a meeting and starting point for such extended research and practice that we believe will be of interest to a wide range of people engaged in language and literacy education. A key audience that is well placed to take up these insights and develop them further is, of course, the teaching professionals at school and university levels, teacher educators and policy-makers concerned with language and diversity issues in education and in society more generally. We also anticipate that researchers working in the fields of English and English Language, English for Academic Purposes, English as an Additional/Second Language, Literacy Studies, Educational Linguistics and Socio/Applied Linguistics (in educational settings) will find the discussion relevant to their concerns, while the rich international diversity of the accounts will appeal to readers interested in seeing beyond their own immediate context.

Index